Using Visual Technology in Educational Ethnography

Introducing readers to debates underpinning the uses of visual technology in educational ethnography, this book takes actual research projects across different country contexts to discuss how research designs can use visual technology in educational ethnography to show connections between theory, method and research problems.

The book begins by introducing readers to three epistemological positions underpinning the use of visual technology in social science and educational research: the scientific realist, reflexive and dialectic. It illustrates the uses of visual technology in the form of digital film and photographs and how, as a source of data, it has potential in developing ethnographic knowledge and representation in a range of educational contexts. The ideas are illustrated through three research projects in the context of classrooms, home environments and intervention work with practitioners. With clear practical applications, this resource considers the part theory plays in research designs, which use visual technology to investigate educational problems.

Using Visual Technology in Educational Ethnography is ideal reading for anyone seeking to learn more about the benefits and practicalities of using visual technology within their ethnographic practice.

Rita Chawla-Duggan is an Associate Professor in Education at the University of Bath, UK.

Qualitative and Visual Methodologies in Educational Research

Series Editors: Rita Chawla-Duggan and Simon Hayhoe, University of Bath, UK

We are increasingly living in an era where students and researchers are under severe time pressures, whilst the amount of research topics, methodologies, data collection methods and ethical questions continue to grow. The *Qualitative and Visual Methodologies in Educational Research* series provides concise, accessible texts that take account of the methodological issues that emerge out of researching educational issues. They are ideal reading for all those designing and implementing unfamiliar qualitative research methods, from undergraduates to the most experienced researchers.

Books in the series:

- Are compact, comprehensive works, to appeal to final year undergraduates and early career postgraduates, at masters and doctoral level – both PhD and EdD. These works can also be easily read and digested by emerging, early career researchers, or raise issues applicable to experienced researchers who are keeping up with their field.
- Reflect on a single methodological problem per volume. In particular, the titles examine data analysis, research design, access, sampling, ethics, the role of theory, and how fieldwork is experienced in real-time.
- Have chapters that discuss the context of education, teaching and learning, and so can include a psychological as well as social and cultural understanding of teaching and learning in non-traditional or non-formal, as well as formal settings.
- Include discussions that engage critically with ontological and epistemological debates underpinning the choice of qualitative or visual methodologies in educational research.

The *Qualitative and Visual Methodologies in Educational Research* series includes books which stimulate ideas and help the reader design important and insightful research that improves the lives of others though education, to ultimately inspire the development of qualitative and visual methodologies.

Titles in the series include:

Qualitative Research Methods in English Medium Instruction for Emerging Researchers
Theory and Case Studies of Contemporary Research
Edited by Samantha Curle and Jack Pun

Using Visual Technology in Educational Ethnography
Theory, Method and the Visual
Rita Chawla-Duggan

For more information about this series, please visit: https://www.routledge.com/Qualitative-and-Visual-Methodologies-in-Educational-Research/book-series/QVMER

Using Visual Technology in Educational Ethnography
Theory, Method and the Visual

Rita Chawla-Duggan

Routledge
Taylor & Francis Group

LONDON AND NEW YORK

First published 2024
by Routledge
4 Park Square, Milton Park, Abingdon, Oxon OX14 4RN

and by Routledge
605 Third Avenue, New York, NY 10158

Routledge is an imprint of the Taylor & Francis Group, an informa business

© 2024 Rita Chawla-Duggan

The right of Rita Chawla-Duggan to be identified as author of this work has been asserted in accordance with sections 77 and 78 of the Copyright, Designs and Patents Act 1988.

All rights reserved. No part of this book may be reprinted or reproduced or utilised in any form or by any electronic, mechanical, or other means, now known or hereafter invented, including photocopying and recording, or in any information storage or retrieval system, without permission in writing from the publishers.

Trademark notice: Product or corporate names may be trademarks or registered trademarks, and are used only for identification and explanation without intent to infringe.

British Library Cataloguing-in-Publication Data
A catalogue record for this book is available from the British Library

ISBN: 978-0-367-42990-4 (hbk)
ISBN: 978-1-032-69535-8 (pbk)
ISBN: 978-1-003-00054-9 (ebk)

DOI: 10.4324/9781003000549

Typeset in Times New Roman
by SPi Technologies India Pvt Ltd (Straive)

For Elliot and Aidan …and... In memory of my father,
Girdhari Lal Chawla, with gratitiude and love

The true mystery of the world is the visible, not the invisible

Oscar Wilde

Contents

List of Figures	ix
List of Tables	xi
About the Author	xii
Acknowledgements	xiii

1 Introduction   1

The structure of the book 7
Setting the scene: From ethnography to educational ethnography 10
Subject–object interdependence 12
Context and holism 13
A methodological approach 13
Process, product, reflexivity and reality 14
Notes 16

2 Visual technology for educational ethnography: Possibilities, positions and potential   17

Introduction 17
Representations of reality and the visual – three ontological and epistemological positions 17
Capturing the dialectic in visual contexts and ethnographic knowledge 40
Conclusion 44
Notes 45

3 Visual technology and invisible pedagogy: Using film and photography to analyse pedagogic culture   46

Introduction 46
Pedagogic cultures through the visual 48

viii Contents

    ICDS pedagogy and visual images: sampling, logging, editing 52
    Combining theory and method 56
    *Visual analysis and pedagogic communication – a structural
       analysis* 57
    *The anganwadi settings and visual analysis of pedagogic
       practice* 58
    *Generating theoretical insights that inform narrative
       accounts* 66
    Conclusion 67

4 Video modalities as a psychological technique: Studying human development qualitatively and its implications for making learner agency visible   69

    Introduction 69
    Video modalities in social science research 70
    The study, video modalities, development and the dialectic 72
    *Case study illustrations of extractive and reflective video
       modalities* 75
    Discussion 83
    *Implications for video modalities and researching
       learner agency* 85
    Conclusion 87
    Notes 87

5 Transformative visual representations in interventionist methodology: Seeing is thinking in the Change Laboratory   89

    Introduction 89
    *Interventions, educational research and Change Lab.
       (CL) methodology* 90
    The study, CHAT and the Change Lab. (CL) 96
    Visual representations and the three screens 101
    The role of the researcher-interventionist 107
    *Methodological reflections and conclusion: the Change
       Lab. as a collaborative visual language of description* 115
    Notes 118

6 Conclusion   119

    Appendix 1: Examples of educational ethnographies   130
    References   132
    Index   141

Figures

2.1	Saraswati	22
2.2	School	22
2.3	School playground	23
2.4	Hometime	23
2.5	Reading to the class	23
2.6	Revising Hindi	23
2.7	Revising with peers	23
2.8	Solving a maths problem with class peers	23
2.9	Getting maths marked	24
2.10a/b	Being class monitor	24
2.10c	Being class monitor	25
2.10d	Being class monitor	25
2.10e	(Right) Being class monitor	25
2.11	Eating lunch with school friends	26
2.12	Eating an ice lolly with a school friend	26
2.13	(a and b) Buying and eating a snack with a school friend	26
2.14	Playing games with friends at lunchtime	26
2.15	Organising a lunchtime game	26
2.16a/b	Sisters doing homework	27
2.17a	Homestead maintenance	27
2.17b	Fuel for the home	27
2.17c	Collecting wood for cooking	28
2.17d	Chopping wood for cooking	28
2.17e/f	Keeping the homestead clear of animals	28
2.17g	Buying groceries with mum	29
2.18a/b	Helping in community	29
2.19a/b	Playing in community	30
2.20a/b	Sitting in community	31
2.21–24	Scene: The woodland walk – video scene extracted from body camera footage	37
2.25	Woodland Walk, Scene: Children watching video to recall (video for recall)	38

x *Figures*

2.26	Woodland Walk, Scene: Teachers watching video to reflect (video for reflection)	38
3.1	Anganwadi 1 – Image from Scene 1 – Reciting rhyme: Munni Behta illustrating strong discursive rules	59
3.2	Anganwadi 1 – Image from Scene 1 – Reciting rhyme illustrating weak classification of space and children's contribution to content selection	60
3.3	Anganwadi 1 – Image from Scene 2 – Tell a story: Marathi	60
3.4	Anganwadi 2 – Image of Wall displays illustrating strong classification between subject knowledge	61
3.5	Anganwadi 2 – Image from Scene 4 – Watch the pointer	62
3.6	(a and b) Anganwadi 3 – Image from Scene – Reciting rhymes	63
3.7	(a and b) Anganwadi 5 – Image from Scene – outside and inside the setting	64
3.8	Anganwadi 5 – Image from Scene – Stacking cups	65
3.9	Anganwadi 6 – Setting up to eat together	66
4.1	Video and Vygotsky Modalities: Video modalities as a psychological technique to study opportunities for development and agency	76
4.2	Norway, Participant footage – Playing games (cards)	77
4.3	Hong Kong, Researcher footage – Video for reflection and accessing children's attention	79
4.4	(a–c) Hong Kong, Researcher footage – Video for reflection and sustaining children's attention	80
4.5	Hong Kong, Researcher footage: Video for reflection and transforming children's reflections through sustained attention	81
5.1	The Activity System with contradictions indicated; adapted from Cole and Engeström 1993: 36	92
5.2	An emotionally charged moment in the Change Laboratory	110
5.3	Activity Theory analysis and the developing object – The process of practitioners' working with groups	114
6.1	Image of international team – negotiation, collaboration and critique of model through shared video footage viewing	123

Tables

1.1 Visual modes and modalities 3
2.1 Educational ethnography and dialectics for the
     purposes of research in education 43
5.1 Practitioners' directions and tensions 100

About the Author

Rita Chawla-Duggan is Associate Professor in Education at the University of Bath. She trained as a teacher and educational ethnographer. Further training in filmmaking for fieldwork broadened her methodological knowledge into visual technology, visual ethnography and post-developmental video methodologies. She works with film makers and illustrators and led a four-country methodological project entitled 'Using Digital Visual methods in Cross Cultural Research'. Her methodological publications are in *Qualitative Research*, the *International Journal of Qualitative Research* and *Pedagogy, Culture and Society*.

Acknowledgements

I am indebted to many colleagues for my interest in approaches to visual ethnography. Special thanks goes to the educational ethnographers at the University of Warwick, with whom I had the good fortune to work at the start of my research career. Much thanks also to the film maker Dr. George Chan for his insights into the film making world.

Thank you also to the AVA department at the University of Bath for their enormous technical help, especially Alan Harris and Lou Piper.

Finally, thanks to Mitali Dutta and Elliot Chawla-Duggan for excellent proof reading. Obviously any errors remain my responsibility.

1 Introduction

The way we see the social world is affected by what we know, which may not always be expressed through words. The process occurs from the very beginning, when 'seeing comes before words', and 'the child looks and recognises before it can speak' (Berger 1972: 7). Herein lies the value of the visual as a mode of understanding human experience. For social science researchers who draw on ethnographic approaches to understanding how human beings experience the social world, knowing how we arrive at that understanding through our research methods is critical to interpreting the emic (or insider) perspective. For those using visuals in research, it raises fundamental questions about the relation between what we look at, as an act of choice, through the visual, and how we explain what is going on. However, using the visual is nothing new in ethnographic research.

Anthropologists Gregory Bateson and Margaret Mead (1942) were pioneers in using film and photography in their ethnographic study of Balinese society. They helped to underscore the importance of visual evidence in ethnography, with books and films achieving seminal status. In many ways they began the field of visual ethnography, but another classically cited academic in the field is John Collier (1967) with his emphasis on analysis and use of photographs in ethnography. His work led to significant contributions in other subfields, especially in the applied anthropology of education. *Visual Anthropology: Photography as a Research Method* (1967) is one of his seminal textbooks still (revised 1986) in use today. Then there is the classic paper *Photography and Sociology* in which the sociologist and ethnographer Howard Becker (1974) provided an exposition about the similar origins and interest of photography and sociology in exploring society, alongside their departures from one another; and in this respect, Becker (1974) laid a foundation for future possibilities. My citations indicate a rich ranging historical landscape of visual ethnography as an approach to research. In the book I take a step forward in time, bringing in digital technology, examining visual technology in ethnographic research, using video and photography. I focus specifically on 'application' in asking the question 'how do social science researchers use visual technology to work on research problems in education, and what possibilities are available for educational ethnography?'

What do I mean methodologically when I refer to visual technology though? Visual technology is, as I see it, a source of data. In that respect it might include several sources: web-based sources, all manner of digital cameras and video film production devices including smartphones, laptops and tablets which are now embedded in our lives, enabling global and more local connections (Hammersley and Atkinson 2019); indeed, anything which incorporates our experiences through the medium of visual technology (for the purposes of research). The value of those sources of visual technology lies in how they and we produce different modes of visual information, in a range of categories, where different modes express themselves through different modalities. There is an argument to say ethnography has always been essentially multimodal, in the ways in which fieldworkers use all senses (Hammersley and Atkinson 2019); but with visual technology educational ethnographers have greater opportunities to build a different kind of social portrait. Modes of visual information might include models, maps, photographs, drawings, architectural plans, films, videos and web pages. They may be in information categories already available for researchers to use or they may be produced by researchers themselves. Alternatively, information may be produced by others at a researcher's request; or may be linked to other information, for example, images linked to texts on the web. In terms of functions, researchers can ask the question, 'what work do different modes do?' Well that too differs according to the purpose of our research. For example, the choice of visual mode being used might function to provide information about: participant's perspectives (especially useful for the non-verbal); accessing aspects of people's lives researchers cannot easily access and observe (for example, home/work life); or even providing ways of recording reflections or live events for analysis (for example, class and curriculum teaching, school events, collaborative professional development). In educational projects researchers increasingly use modes of images and films to function as stimulus material for interviews and focus groups. Functions might also include allowing participants to *show* you their world, not only *tell*; expressing thoughts, feelings and emotions; revealing deeper meanings; uncovering underlying structures; showing power structures, gender bias and racial prejudice; and discovering unconscious and difficult to reach processes by 'making the invisible visible' (Barry, 1994: 37). The process of making a drawing on an iPad, for example, might function to allow participants to 'share different things, that would not have been shared if they had been asked to describe their experience verbally' (Kearney and Hyle, 2004: 375). Additionally, certain modes may allow you to gain insights into social functions of the 'cultural product', for example, as do advertisements and social media apps. Instagram and TikTok are examples of social media apps dedicated to the function of photo and video sharing, created for and consumed by users. Such modes may also help gain understanding and insight about the broader aspects of society such as the values and norms of a culture.

Table 1.1 lists several visual modes. Reflect on each of them, considering their purposes in terms of functions or modalities.

Throughout the book I aim to facilitate a critical understanding about problems, possibilities and the potential of using visual technology to study educational problems. Additionally, I introduce key epistemological and ontological positions underpinning the use of visual in ethnographic or ethnographic-oriented research. The book aims to first position the use of visual technology in research designs, so it is theoretically linked to educational problems. Second, the book presents research designs, which are practically useful, in a range of educational contexts. I focus on

Table 1.1 Visual modes and modalities

Modes	Modalities (*How is it expressed and for what purpose?*)
• Artefacts/objects, e.g., models and charts	How have you seen models used in social science research?
• Maps	How have you seen maps used by educational researchers? (See, for example, Donnelly 2016 in his study of higher education trajectories)
• Photographs	How do studies use photo elicitation? (see, for example, Chawla-Duggan's examples in Chapter 2 of her childhood ethnography of schooling in India)
• Drawings/architectural plans	How have you seen architectural drawings used by educational researchers? (See, for example, Daniels et al. 2022 in a study of school buildings)
• Films/Videos	For video – how have you seen it used in sports programmes? (For reflection?) Could this be used with teachers? (See Chapter 4 with reference to video modalities)
• Web pages	See, for example, Limin Gu (2017) in the study of using school websites for home–school communication and parental involvement
• Graffiti and murals	Social science researchers use Graffiti and street art research (GSAR) to study urban space (see, for example, Fransberg et al. (2021). How might educational researchers use this approach in their research?
• Eye-tracking	How has eye-tracking been used in studies of autism, learning and to identify disadvantages in learning opportunities? (See, for example, Moore et al. 2018)

illustrating how I used visual technology in the modes of digital video film and photographs, and I demonstrate how, as a source of data, visual technology has huge potential in addressing educational problems and developing ethnographic knowledge, in a range of contexts.

Specifically, the objectives for the book are to:

1 introduce philosophical positions underpinning the use of visual in research generally, to address educational problems and develop ethnographic knowledge about and for education;
2 explicate the relationship between problem and theory in research designs using visual technology as a source of data in ethnographic-oriented studies, drawing on project material; and
3 reflect on the potential of using visual technology as a reflexive and dialectic source in producing ethnographic-oriented studies, in a range of educational contexts.

Philosophical positions underpinning the use of visual in education and social science research are not always explicated in visual methods literature, yet there are important epistemological questions to consider. For example, what kind of knowledge and knowing is being produced when we use visual methods in educational research? And when it comes to 'truth', what are the associated ontological assumptions influencing the way we come to know, and in turn how we collect and analyse visual material to produce ethnographic knowledge in education?

The question of 'truth' is beautifully illustrated and discussed in Berger's (1972) classic text 'Ways of seeing'. Berger's book is about how to look at art, examining the hidden and not so hidden meanings of paintings and the act of looking. The cover famously reproduced the surrealist painter René Magritte's seminal work about the problem of representation, from a painting entitled 'The Key to Dreams'[1]. And the problem of representation is a key concern for social science researchers too, when they consider the relationship between word, image and meaning. Indeed, Rose (2017), reflecting historically on 'Ways of Seeing' in an art blog, wrote:

> Word and image rapidly became bi-polar nodes of consciousness at the onset of the 20th century, accelerated by the widespread use of the camera, mid-century world wars, a concurrent rise of popular science and psychology, and the breakdown of belief in almost every sphere. It was only logical that the notion of the thing and its name would be viewed as an essentially arbitrary relationship... Words are plastic; meaning and truth are subjective... In their work, both Magritte (1898–1967) and Berger bang up again and again against the stubbornness of the object – the idea of objective reality.
>
> (2017)

The problem of representation and truth lies in presenting us as the audience and viewer, with an absurd mix of contrasting words, images and meaning in the 'The Key to Dreams'. Here, certain mismatched words label a series of images ... so, for example, we see an image of a horse, labelled as 'the door'. We are left with questions about meaning and how we might explain the image. It is through such absurdity that the viewer is introduced to the problem of representation, interpretation and 'truth', and deeper ontological questions of how reality is represented:

> ...meaning, one realizes, is ultimately in flux. ...Berger and Magritte charge the viewer with the responsibility of working out the real, and ultimately that which is critical and consequential. How to do that, how to decode reality?
>
> (Rose 2017)

The 'decoding of reality', which carries its own ontological assumptions, is not only the preoccupation of art critics, but is of central concern for social science and educational researchers and, most certainly, educational ethnographers.

Philosophical positions can, I believe, be brought into practical reality when researchers consider the role of theory in research designs. The relationship is fundamental to academic research. Indeed, I would maintain that a key problem, however, is how we explain the relationship between theory, the visual and research. Seminal advice given to social science researchers states what not to do when grappling with theory in research:

> ...Avoid any rigid set of procedures...avoid the fetishism of method and technique...let theory and method again become part of the practice of a craft.
>
> (Wright Mills, 1959: 224)

But if we separate theory from research, do we lose our ability to explain what the research means? In 'The role of theory in field research', Burgess (1982/2015) provided an account of how researchers consider the part theory plays in field research. Beginning with an assumption, namely, that a key problem in sociology and social anthropology is about the relationship between theory and research, Burgess (1982/2015) demonstrated how existing debates in the 1980s suggested that the linear methodological processes depicted in the sciences, which acted as a frame of reference for proposing scientific rigour in the social sciences, were, in fact, misleading. This is because the research process in natural sciences which leads to key developments is seldom void of social and political struggles (see, for example, the work of Latour and Woolgar 1979 on how scientific work is conducted). For those readers who have not seen the film *The Race for the*

6   *Introduction*

Double Helix (1987) based on Watson's (1968) memoir, Burgess (1982) cites Crick and Watson's discovery of the structure of DNA to illustrate his point:

> Here, we are made aware that research does not occur in 'stages' and does not follow a linear path, but instead is a social process, in which overlap occurs between all areas of the investigation…if we are to understand the research process, it is essential to grasp how theory is interrelated with methods of research, observations, generalisations and hypothesis.
>
> (1982: 209)

How then is theory interrelated with visual methods of data collection and for what purpose? In addressing the question, I maintain a general thread through the book, which is about the importance of the relationship between theory and method. I draw on three examples of projects using visual technology as the source of data for ethnographic oriented research designs, to address three main educational problems, all of which address the role of theory in research designs, using visual technology as a source of data. Those educational problems are about researching and understanding meanings about:

- Classroom pedagogy and cultures of settings
- Learning and child development
- Collaborative intervention-based professional development.

Visual technology and the forms of potential visual data they provided served different functions in each of those studies. In the study of classroom pedagogy, digital camera and video film provided photographs and film footage to shed light on the culture of classroom environments; in the study of learning and development, I used digital film footage to explicate data which shed light on how development happens and the opportunities for child development afforded through interactions, where the non-verbal was a key aspect of age-related adult–child interactions. Finally, three visual screens representing a heuristic diagram, reflections and ethnographic data in a researcher intervention project demonstrated how professional development happens, through an expansion of learning. In the latter example, the visual forms functioned to facilitate methodological understanding of spatial thought as a contribution to linguistic thought in the way a Change Laboratory (CL) intervention methodology is set up. The book therefore has clear practical applications in the field of education and its range of contexts for teachers, learners and practitioners, whilst also discussing the part theory plays in research designs using visual technology as a source of data for educational ethnography, to address educational problems.

Introduction 7

The structure of the book

The book contains six chapters, including this introduction. A short introductory sub-section in this chapter also familiarises readers with historical origins and debates about what we mean by educational ethnography. It also serves as a basis for the follow-up chapter which looks specifically at visual technology and how it can map onto and extend educational ethnography, in terms of its philosophical assumptions.

Chapter 2: *Visual technology for educational ethnography: Possibilities, positions and potential*

Chapter 2 introduces the reader to debates and epistemological positions underpinning the use of visual technology in social science and educational research. The positions I introduce are the scientific realist, the reflexive and the dialectic. Several authors challenge the kind of naïve empiricism accompanying the first position, as it characterises the visual as an objective means of representation (Banks 2001, Banks and Zeitlyn 2015, Buckingham 2009, Pink 2021). The opponents firmly argue that since visual representations are always constructed, they should not be seen as a means of objectively documenting reality. The second, a reflexive position, moves away from traditional ideas of knowledge production associated with scientific realism. From this position, using photography and video recording solely to 'collect data' overlooks the value of visual ambiguity. It is consequently a way of being open to many ways of knowing, and to exploring and reflecting on new routes to knowledge. When we practise this as researchers, the relationship between seeing and knowing becomes exciting, as more possibilities are opened. A third position currently used in the study of educational problems is the dialectic (Fleer 2014b; Engeström 1987/2015). Dialectics is understood here in a Hegelian sense (see Hegel 1807/1977) as a theoretically informed mechanism of movement in the development of consciousness. It elucidates the contradictions existing in the very nature of thought (cf. Tolman 2001) as part of the movement of thinking. Through the notion of dialectic, in accordance with Vygotsky's proposal that psychological work requires the study of the process of change (Vygotsky 1987: 64–65), visual technology in the form of digital video film footage can function to capture the dynamics of change as movement, particularly in studies relating to the field of human development.

Chapter 3: *Visual technology and invisible pedagogy: Using film and photography to understand pedagogic culture*

In Chapter 3 I show how an orientation towards the study of processes rather than simply focusing on the image allows researchers to study 'symbols' semiotically, as an analytic tool (see Chandler cited in Prosser and Loxley 2008). The chapter draws on a study using visual technology to explore the 'symbols' which semiotically make up a culture of preschool settings. Visual data in this form might be of interest in understanding pre-school pedagogy, precisely because pre-school activities do not always look like organised pedagogy, as Bernstein's (1975) use of the term 'invisible' implied. When examining productions of pedagogic practices which lead to learning, Bernstein located the kinds of messages existing in English primary schools in the 1960s by examining thirty-six photographs included in the influential Plowden Report (an illustration of child-centred progressive schooling in England at the time). The point Bernstein (1990/2003) illustrated was how, in the photographs, whilst there may not be an explicitly visible hierarchy between teacher and pupil, there is an implicit one at work; it is one which creates the context described. In this respect, he argued, the photographs showed a desired culture of teaching and learning, where the teacher's power acts directly on the context of learning, rather than upon the students themselves.

In the study recalled in Chapter 3, visual data functioned as a way of gaining orientation into the culture of pre-school slum settings in a district of Mumbai, and I used the data to analyse pedagogic practice. Forms of visual data included digital photographs of blackboards, poster displays and film footage of interaction and activities in six pre-school slum settings in Mumbai, India. The chapter discusses the process of sampling, editing and analysis of visual data, alongside other kinds of data, to generate theoretical insights that informed narrative accounts of pedagogic culture.

Chapter 4: Video modalities as a psychological technique: Studying human development qualitatively

Chapter 4 discusses methodological issues and a technique using two video modalities to understand children's 'social situation of development'. This is a key concept underpinning the work of Vygotsky (1998a, 1998b) from cultural-historical psychology and its view of human development, and a way of explicating a child's (or the subject's) perspective, in terms of his/her object-oriented motive. The data draws from a study entitled 'Using Digital Visual Methods in Cross National Research with Young Children'. The aims of the study were primarily methodological, in that it aimed to test out the affordances of using digital visual technology to examine learning as it develops through interaction, from the child's perspective. In the study, visual technology refers to a range of filmmaking devices, used to produce digital film footage and photographs,

Introduction 9

generated by children and families. In the study we used a Vygotskian concept of development, in which development is not already formed. This kind of perspective on human development requires methodological tools which enable researchers to document human development in a qualitative way. The chapter demonstrates how we found video modalities hold possibilities to do this, because they enable researchers to hone in on the dynamics and conditions for change, and consequently for identifying opportunities for development.

Chapter 5: Transformative visual representations in interventionist methodology: Seeing is thinking in the Change Laboratory

Chapter 5 discusses a study aimed to facilitate practitioner or professional learning and development by practically implementing Engeström's (2007) 'Change Laboratory' (CL) technique. As a research approach, CL is well documented as applied research in interventionist studies of transformation in work (Engeström, Lompscher and Rückriem 2005; Engeström 2008). What is not so well documented is the part visual representations play in CL; specifically, how they work together and for what function, to facilitate an interventionist methodology, for collaborative learning, and change in professional practice.

Rooted in the cultural historical activity theory tradition (CHAT), the perspective underpinning the Change Lab. approach poses the kinds of questions associated with the development of self(ves) within social practice. As a theory it offers a historically grounded account of how transformative collective practices produce and are produced through social interaction and human selves. As a method, the Change Lab. aims to develop work practices, to be used by a team of practitioners with the help of an interventionist (Engeström 2007). In Chapter 5 I discuss a research and development project about supporting practitioners' work in paternal involvement. In Phase 1 of the study, ethnographic case studies explored the ways in which practitioners interpreted and supported paternal involvement. Phase 2, the development stage, used the 'Change Lab.' as development work research (DWR) in the form of workshops. The chapter discusses how different forms of visual representations used in DWR workshops worked together to facilitate shifts in problematising thinking about practitioner work practice. I demonstrate how practitioners were able to think about their work through the visual representations themselves, enabling them to expand linguistic explanations about their work activity problem, in terms of its context, social processes and potential for change. In this respect, I also found CL to be a rare example of mixed methods research, mixed in a qualitatively driven way (Mason 2006).

Chapter 6: Conclusion

The final chapter of the book provides a summary and reflections of methodological issues raised throughout the book, asking the reader to reflect on their methodological imagination for future possibilities of using visual technology in educational ethnography, in increasingly digitised, material educational environments.

Setting the scene: From ethnography to educational ethnography

Rooted in social anthropology and strongly influenced by the Chicago School of Sociology, modern ethnography is a major field of education, with several seminal school-based studies dedicated to its development since the 1960s in the UK,[2] for example, in the work of Hargreaves (1967), Lacey (1970) and Lambart (1976, 1982, 1997). These early UK studies arose out of a research programme based in the Department of Social Anthropology and Sociology at the University of Manchester, applying an anthropological approach to the study of three schools, relying on participation observation as the central method of data collection: Lacey's research was of a boys' grammar school, Lambart's was a girls' grammar school and Hargreaves' was a boys' senior school (Beach et al. 2018: 173). Another important contribution in the UK was from the Birmingham Centre for Contemporary Cultural Studies (CCCS), producing Paul Willis' seminal education ethnography 'Learning to Labour' (1977). The centre was known for applying a Marxist and later feminist approach to study 'culture'. Willis' study focussed on the notion of a 'counterculture' in schools, arising amongst working class boys in a secondary modern school, its relationship with the culture of their parents (Willis 1977), and how it worked to channel the boys into working class jobs, and therefore reproducing the social order associated with capitalist-oriented societies (Beach et al. 2018: 176).

Ethnographic studies involve the study of different cultures; they involve understanding meaning and action and are concerned with getting at the emic, by which I mean an insider's perspective. Methodologists locate the approach within traditions of 'verstehen' and an interpretivist paradigm (Hammersley and Atkinson 2019). Epistemologically, the kinds of knowledge ethnographies subsequently produce stand in contrast to traditions emphasising objective accounts of social reality. Instead, ethnographies recognise the subjective reality of human beings and their experiences, assuming they both constitute and construct the social world.

Traditionally ethnographies are associated with lone anthropologists journeying to small, isolated communities in unfamiliar parts of the world, where they take up residence for an extended period. Their purpose

Introduction 11

is to describe the life of people in as much detail as possible. Through description they aim to reveal a social portrait of culture. Culture, a key concept in social and socio-cultural anthropology, is complex. Defined in several ways, it may be considered to comprise many aspects; the social, structural, political, economic, technological, ethical, spiritual and ideological. Rather than begin with a hypothesis or a structured data collection procedure to follow, ethnographers bring along an often implicit list of the aspects of culture usually described in a completed ethnography, a set of analytical categories normally found in an ethnographer's vocabulary, and a concern for certain broad questions about culture which they know will be discussed, when they return from the field. In developing their cultural descriptions, ethnographers commonly engage in activities which include participant and non-participant observation, informal and formal interviews, document analysis and various non-obtrusive measures (Webb et al. 1966). The data collected in fieldwork are traditionally recorded in field notes which are later coded and analysed to produce the final product, an ethnography. The ethnography will include narrative accounts of events and series of events along with a discussion of the meanings of these events to the members of the community. Also included will be more analytical treatments of various topics which seem to capture what is distinctive about the culture observed.

Historically, ethnography evolved as an approach to research used by social anthropologists to observe and study non-industrial communities. Bronisław Malinowski was a Polish-born anthropologist who pioneered participant observation as an ethnographic method. His time spent living among the Trobriand Islanders on the Trobriand Islands in New Guinea gave him a unique perspective on ethnography, one which came to influence later generations of anthropologists (see Malinowski 1922/2014). Anthropologists then turned their attention to their own urban cultures and to focus on settings and activities in urban environments. Anthropology, for example, influenced the seminal work of the Chicago School of Urban Sociology. In the area of education, a burgeoning interest in the ethnography of educational settings resulted in filling a gap for longitudinal, qualitative and open-ended research, whilst, at the same time, acknowledging the central importance of education as part of culture. Longitudinal information in ethnographies helps us to understand process and change, and this can be especially revealing for understanding culture in relation to educational problems, and in seeing, for example, qualitative or structural changes within culture. This is a dynamic view of culture, seen as an ongoing process rather than an accomplished fact. In contemporary discussions, educational ethnographers recognise this feature, defining the term 'ethnography' in several ways (see Hammersley and Atkinson 2019). Hammersley (2006), for example, gave recognition to its variation and use, by using a notion of 'ethnographic dimensions'. Those dimensions include:

- the kinds of methods employed: these may be solely based on qualitative enquiry such as case study or combined with quantitative data.
- its methodological orientation: this emphasises the importance of studying 'at first hand' what people do and say.
- and 'context', whether it is micro or macro, construed or discovered, and how its relationship to theory is presented.

Whilst Hammersley's (2006) conceptualisation of ethnography recognises variation and use, the epistemological and ontological assumptions underpinning the dimensions remain implicit. I would say there are two principal assumptions of ethnographic knowledge:

1 ethnographic knowledge assumes a subject–object interdependence and
2 ethnographic knowledge assumes context is equated with a holistic social portrait of the phenomena under study.

Subject–object interdependence

In any given cultural situation, ethnography values both the 'insider's' and researcher's interpretations. The terms 'emic' and 'etic' taken from linguistics correspond to these two interpretations. In this way ethnographers recognise the native and researcher's perspective as essential knowledge about a given culture. They avoid treating subjects as objects, aiming instead to value their experience as expertise. At the same time in taking the role of participant observer, attempting to combine in one individual both the insider and outsider perspective, they maintain a dialectic between their own emic and etic perspective (Wax 1971). By including both these perspectives, ethnographers recognise how, ontologically speaking, there are multiple interpretations of the same reality. Whilst ethnographers might aim to gather the emic perspective to explain activities in which they engage or courses of action they adopt, they also emphasise the analytic perspective on activities and actions (Hammersley 2006), the etic perspective. A tension can exist between the two perspectives, that is, the participant perspective and analytic perspective of the ethnographer (Hammersley 2006). This in part relates to the assumption that ethnographic knowledge and its attention to subjectivity diminishes any understanding of what is really 'out there' (Bassey 1999). Ethnographers continuously grapple with subject–object understanding (in the sense of 'whose' perspective will be used to explain their cultural reality). In line with this assumption, ethnographic knowledge might document the perspectives of participants with varying roles and statuses within the same setting (see, for example, Burgess 1984). Ideally multiple emic and

Introduction 13

etic interpretations are overlaid to provide a 'thick description' (Geertz, 1973) of the same cultural scenes.

Context and holism

Holism is a second epistemological assumption in ethnographic knowledge. Ethnographers study culture. Cultural phenomena is studied holistically in its context. If they study one aspect of a culture, for example, child rearing, then that aspect is examined in context, one in which all other aspects of the culture are related to it. Put another way, there may be a system and it exists as a part of several systems, which help to explain the culture. This is a form of holism. Whether an ethnographer expects to locate what is being studied in the context of wider society, or whether s/he decides to concentrate on studying in detail what people do in particular local contexts (Hammersley 2006, 6) is also debated in terms of what constitutes ethnographic knowledge. In response, I would say we cannot really understand what goes on within situations unless its explanation is located within a broader social context. Class, age, gender, religion and ethnicity are all examples of 'what is out there' and are structural conditions both governing and constituting at the same time, how members of a given society interact with one another. As such they are part of the holistic picture the ethnographer paints. So, simply because an account stress situated meaning and context does not mean it diminishes the importance of structure. In fact, being concerned with context ensures that any explanation about social action takes account of structural conditions that may shape, limit and, in some cases, define the social action (Pole and Morrison 2003). It may also highlight how ethnography's troubled relations between subjectivity and structure (as an emic and etic) are in an evolving inter-dependence, representing reality.

The principle of holism leads to qualitative narratives which describe thick slices of life reflecting culture; and in this respect the visual, especially digital video and film, has much to offer. It is a valuable component for the ethnographer because the use of digital video and film allows researchers to construct whole pieces of cultural data. In Chapter 2, I explore its use and the question of whether using visual, and especially video, in research is to be considered as simply a 'supplement' or whether it has so much more to offer as a source of 'potential and possibilities' for the educational ethnographer and ethnographic knowledge.

A methodological approach

Whilst ethnography is probably most well known as a methodological approach to experiencing, interpreting and representing culture and society, it is also a process of creating and representing knowledge, based on the ethnographer's experience (Pink 2021). By implication, the perspective aligns itself with an ontological positioning, one that pertains not to produce or create an objective or universally truthful account of reality, but versions of reality intertwined with the ethnographers' experiences alongside social, political, ethical and spiritual beliefs about reality. Pink (2021) insists those experiences offer a version of reality that is 'as loyal as possible to the context, the embodied, sensory, and affective experiences, and the negotiations and intersubjectivities through which knowledge was produced' (40).

Aligned with this ontological positioning about truth are certain methods, which include reflexive, participative and collaborative approaches to research. Informants might be involved in a variety of ways, at different times in the study, and the account would be an observable record of realities, in the form of field notes, texts, objects, images, the material and sensory characteristics of knowledge and experience.

In characterising ethnography, it is also important to grapple with the question of representation. This involves a consideration of certain questions about the right of the researcher to represent other people (Pink 2021: 40), recognising the impossibility of knowing other minds (Fernandez 1995). Given, we can never really know what someone is really thinking; the nearest we might get in grappling with representation may also mean acknowledging how the sense we make of informants' words and actions is actually 'an expression of our own consciousness' (Cohen and Rapport 1995: 12).

So, it seems there is no clear-cut answer about what makes an activity, image or knowledge ethnographic. A single representation is not ethnographic, but we might say the 'ethnographicness' becomes visible when connected to context and a process of interpretation. For Pink (2021) the connection lies in situation, interpretation and use, in which ... the ethnographicness of any image or representation is contingent on how it is situated, interpreted and used to invoke meanings and knowledge that are of ethnographic interest (Pink 2021: 41). And sometimes it can be difficult to see the dividing line between ethnographies and fiction. In the same way, when it comes to photographs, it is difficult to know when a photograph is for a tourist, film documentary or newspaper, or deciding whether a video is home based or ethnographic (Pink 2021).

Process, product, reflexivity and reality

Pole (2004) made distinctions between process and product when discussing ethnography and methodology. For Pole (2004) it does not matter what methods researchers use (as there are ethnographers who also use surveys) as long as the product is a naturalistic account, retaining its 'ethnographicness'. This implies we need to critically reflect on the process of production asking the question, how was the product produced?

> We need to go beyond the possible source of data to include the ways in which the researcher works with the source and the data it might yield.
>
> (Pole 2004)

Pole's request to the social science researcher is connected to a concept of reflexivity:

> ...where the scholar is studying a setting, a subculture, an activity or some actors other than herself, and is acutely sensitive to the interrelationship(s) between herself and the focus of the research.
>
> (Delamont 2009: 58)

Critical discussions about the problem of reflexivity maintain it involves far more than questions of bias, or how ethnographers in observing the reality of a society distort it through their participation. Nor is it a way of neutralising subjectivity through an engagement with how a researcher's presence may affect the reality observed and in turn the data yielded. For Pink (2021) it is tokenistic to assume that a reflexive approach helps ethnographers to produce objective data and wrongly supposes subjectivity could (or should) be avoided or eradicated. Ethnographers do set out to acknowledge their subjectivity as central to ethnographic knowledge. This acknowledgement does not necessarily mean, however, we should abandon all forms of realism in our search for ethnographic understanding. It simply entails acknowledging an awareness of how reality is interpreted and represented.

From this point of view experiencing the social reality of people's lives intertwines with the construction of ethnographic text. Given this position is vulnerable to avoiding how the relationship is fused with the ethnographers' subjectivity, we might propose there is an intersubjective construction of knowledge represented through the ethnographic product. In this respect, the relationship between the subjectivities of the researcher and informants produces a negotiated version of reality.

Clearly to view the ethnographic product as an intersubjective construction of knowledge has implications for the open mindedness of a researcher to another's subjective reality and the extent to which the account becomes less negotiated through subjective understanding. It becomes particularly complex when fused with intersectional social characteristics such as a researcher's or informant's race, gender, class, nationality, religious or spiritual inclination as part of the context created through the activities of the research process. This is a highly complex set of relations. Their complexity is one in which subjective perceptions have implications for the knowledge produced though the interaction between the researcher and informants. In a sense the final ethnography does not aim to give a final answer to research questions. Instead, its goal is the 'enlargement of the universe of discourse' (Geertz 1973) and an exercise in posing increasingly refined questions.

In more contemporary versions of ethnography, there are virtual ethnographies (see Hine 2000) in which ethnographic research is conducted online. This eclectic, electronic space on the internet creates the contemporary 'field' which, we can say, is a space for looking at social processes, practices and relationships in a range of contexts. In education, particularly during and with the impact of COVID-19, our assumptions about the extent to which we saw and experienced social reality as something which was fixed became more visible, in most institutions, as we constructed another version of reality through online spaces in platforms such as Zoom and MS Teams. In a sense, the idea that human beings construct social reality and can impose the way we all arrive at perceiving our social world became more visible than ever, with the use of visual technology. It is the possibilities of making the invisible visible, to which I turn in Chapter 2, as part of examining the possibilities, position and potential of visual technology as a source of data for educational ethnographers.

Notes

1 'The Key to Dreams' is also called 'La Clef des Songes' and refers to the 1930 painting, which included different objects and words in French; the 1935 version in English is slightly different and appeared on John Berger's book cover.
2 Appendix 1 provides references for the ethnographic studies cited in the chapter and an exemplar range of ethnographic studies in educational research.

2 Visual technology for educational ethnography
Possibilities, positions and potential

Introduction

The chapter examines possibilities, positions and potential for using visual technology in educational ethnography. In doing so, it discusses relationships between epistemological and ontological positions, as well as data collection, analysis and dissemination of visual material from digital video film and photography. The chapter encourages educational researchers to reflect upon different modes of visual technology for educational ethnographies.

Epistemological questions about knowledge and how to get at knowledge are all questions underpinned by notions of truth about social reality and what we believe reality to be. In the chapter I introduce three philosophical positions and their connections to visual technology to produce ethnographic knowledge from digital video and photographs. The chapter aims to help researchers critically reflect upon different representations of reality and the potential for producing those representations of reality through ethnographic knowledge, using photography and video whilst also reflecting on the possibilities of other modes of visual technology.

Representations of reality and the visual – three ontological and epistemological positions

Historically, debates surrounding ethnographers using visual as a source of data pivoted on questions about truth and representation, whether data was objective and whether scientific rigour underpinned claims to truth. For the 20 years between the 1960s and 1980s social science methodologists concerned themselves with questions about whether the visual could support observational aspects of projects. At this time, critiques about using the visual in ethnography homed in on the idea that, as a data collection method, the visual remained unrepresentative and unsystematic. Ethnographers like Mead (1975), Collier Jr (1967) and Becker (1974) responded to critiques, both theoretically and in terms of their practical applications and implications, for the use of photography and film in fieldwork. For Mead (1975), on a practical level, if researchers were to produce a more scientifically rigorous and more objective use of the visual, it was important for researchers to leave the camera on, without interference (Mead 1975: 9–10). This kind of approach represented a basis towards a more scientific realist perspective to using visuals in ethnographic studies.

Scientific realism and visual representation

The realist use of photography and film provides an important layer of knowledge in ethnographic texts with the work of Collier and Collier (1986) being seminal in scientific realism. The basis of scientific approaches to visual research was about an ability to translate the visual into words. Most importantly it involved taking the visual and turning it into the verbal through a systematic process of analysis. This is a process aligned with the scientific process to produce claims to a truth which '…involves abstraction of the visual evidence so we can intellectually define what we have recorded and what the visual evidence reveals' (Collier and Collier 1986: 169–170). From this perspective it is not necessary for images to appear in the final piece of research, 'except as occasional illustration' (ibid.). In this respect, the visual is said to support verbal explanations. Consequently, the perspective assumes that whilst we can use visual sources to gather ethnographic information, ethnographic knowledge is produced by translating the visual into written text. The visual remains positioned as a supporting act, one which supports a dominant written text, to communicate ethnographic knowledge.

- *The scientific realist view of knowledge and its relation to context*

In ethnographic studies, context is everything. A scientific realist approach to knowledge aims to regulate context. In Pink's (2007) early seminal writing, she interestingly explained how visual ethnography can use a scientific realist perspective in which context is worked with in two ways. First, scientific realism considers the content of images as important, and so it provides information about activities, individuals and objects represented in images. Researchers then use this knowledge to contextualise information they gather. Second, scientific realism will regulate the content in which the image is produced. Doing this allows the perspective to validate how representative its content is. The perspective not only ensures validity but also reliability, because the procedures are thought to create conditions for replicability in analysis of the visual evidence. This is because 'the significance of what we find in analysis is shaped by the context established by systematic recording during fieldwork, which is contextually complete and sequentially organised' (Collier and Collier 1986: 163).

These kinds of issues enable this perspective to be viewed as one that maintains scientific rigour. The perspective also assumes that, in ethnography, visual images or their content are the object of analysis. In response to this position, Pink (2007) raised two concerns about a scientific realist approach to what we can know about the visual: its assumptions about context and its narration of events. She argued the perspective assumes context may be complete and closed; and that 'the sequence determined by a series of photographs or video produced by the ethnographer represents the relative narrative of events or the key set of actors' (Pink 2007: 122). The concern Pink (2007) raised in relation to this latter assumption is in response to a claim made by Collier and Collier, namely that their technique allows ethnographers to 'record one whole view of culture' (Cited in Pink 2007: 122). Pink questioned this claim on the grounds of a general understanding that ethnographic truths are only ever partial and incomplete (Clifford 1986). To raise both strengths and weaknesses of scientific realism as a perspective for using the visual, Pink (2007) cited Collier and Collier's (1986) seminal case study about 'photographing technology' and maintained how:

> One could argue that a series of photographs that record a process represent only one standpoint of weaving technology, and moreover, in isolating this technological process, decontextualizing it from other important elements of weaving. In short, rather than being complete, the visual record is inevitably partial. ...It is a representation of weaving...
>
> (Pink 2007: 122)

And when analysing the images from this perspective:

> ...analysis of their visual content would not be an objective analysis of a truthful visual record, but one (academic) gaze interpreting a subjective (even if collaborative) visual narrative.
>
> (Pink 2007: 123)

Collier and Collier's (1986) study was about depicting the weaving culture of Otavalo Indians in Ecuador, and it is essentially a study photographing a technology of textiles. In their account of the study the researchers maintained '... we were faced with the problem of having incomplete knowledge about the technology of this area' (Collier and Collier 1986: 71). The researchers consequently set out to gather a more complete ethnographic knowledge through collaboration; and in their book they describe an interesting intersubjective process they underwent to arrive at a truth. Pink's (2007) critique of their work was therefore also partial. Her critique focused on the study representing one version of truth, and in doing so, she gave limited attention to the collaborative processes she acknowledged in their work. In reading their text, the collaborative process is shown to be fundamental to how they gathered and arrived at their ethnographic knowledge. At first, they 'witness the weaver involved in the first part of the textile process – the washing, the drying and the carding of the raw wool' (73). They then showed the weaver their photographs and describe his response:

> He spread the contact prints out on the ground, arranged the pictures in technological sequence, and surveyed our results. He stood up, shook his head in disappointment and made it clear that we had not done a good job on his craft. And more, he said, he was very concerned that the world would see him in these photographs as a poor weaver.... he insisted that we repeat the process ....he made it clear that this time he would let us know *when* to take the pictures....When we returned with our prints a second time, he accepted them with approval, and we proceeded on to the other steps – carding, spinning, and dying the yarn, and finally weaving the cloth.
>
> (Collier and Collier 1986: 73)

Collier and Collier (1986) eventually photographed the master weaver and discussed the quality and content of the photographs with him and, in doing so, recorded the weaving process. He became their key informant, helping them to document the work and technology of other weavers.

> The co-operation of our Indian collaborator allowed us to make a study of the Otavalo textile industry more complete than we ever could have made if we had tried to direct the course of his photographic coverage.
>
> (ibid.)

They describe their experience 'as an acted-out interview stimulated by the feedback of the photographs', arguing 'if the subjects of the study have the initiative of organising and informally directing the fieldworker's observations, the result can be a very complete and authentic record' (Collier and Collier 1986: 73–74). In this respect Collier and Collier (1986) provide a strong argument of how to use photography as a collaborative endeavour in the ethnographic process of data collection, as part of a scientific realist perspective.

Remaining critical of Colliers' work, Pink (2007) maintained it allows ethnographers to 'record one whole view of culture' (ibid.), and this then influences how we see ethnographic truth. For example, in their data collection process they say 'process must be photographed so exact steps can be isolated. It is by this systematic observation that a technology can be conceived functionally' (Collier and Collier 1986: 69). For Pink (2007), however, what is more important is for researchers to remain alert to the possibility that a series of photographs which record a process has both advantages and disadvantages. It 'represents only one standpoint' and that 'isolating' this technology process decontextualises it from other important elements of weaving:

> Isolating the stages of a generalised version of a technological process in this way can provide an abstract or ideal model of that process. Nevertheless, this cannot be a complete or authentic record. Rather it is a representation of weaving.
>
> (Pink 2007: 123)

Pink's critique of course raises fundamental questions about 'who's truth' and 'through who's eyes do we as researchers represent truth?' The social science debate is essentially about the *crisis of representation*. The phrase refers to claims that social researchers are unable to directly represent or depict the lived experiences of people they study. In 1986 George Marcus and Michael Fischer (1986) brought social scientists' attention to the phrase *crisis of representation*; the 1970s and early 1980s methodological backdrop to this was a debate about how boundaries of social science and humanities were becoming blurred in many anthropological writings, by being seen as interpretations of interpretations. My feeling is that today, the crisis of representation as a 'crisis' has more of a historical than contemporary interest. Although researchers still address the problem of representing others or speaking for others, the sense of crisis has diminished. This is because ideas such as acknowledging the importance of subjectivity and the view that objectivity is not entirely possible have become widely accepted by social researchers. Accordingly, the task for social science researchers now is to elaborate on and explore the implications of such realisations. It is in this sense Lincoln and Denzin (2005) choice of documenting the history of qualitative research in the USA through a series of moments (each propelling the next) interestingly noted 'the crisis of representation' as a mark of a fourth moment. This is when qualitative researchers realised they could no longer directly capture lived experience, but that lived experience is created in social texts written by the researcher. Despite criticism to their historicising (see Hammersley 1999), what Denzin and Lincoln's (2005) historical moments do is to capture some of the key transformations and ontological orientations in social/educational research, which fall under the umbrella of qualitative research.

In terms of changing ontological positions about the visual then, Pink's (2007) earlier texts can be located within the moment of 'crisis of representation', in that, even if we regulate how we visually record the context of a process, its content and chronology of the images will not 'represent' a reliable, complete and truthful account. From this

22 Visual technology for educational ethnography

perspective, historical explanations of analysing visual content demonstrate how it is not an objective analysis, but one interpretation and representation of reality. In this respect, scientific realist approaches to documentary photography are informed by 'a' representation of reality, one which often interprets images by their content and chronology.

The implications of this claim are twofold. First, the classic norms of objectivity, truth as correspondence, are no longer applicable to our understanding of inquiry. Second, in response to the demise of these ideas, there is a further understanding that the lived experiences of people are not discovered by researchers to be depicted as they really are; rather, these experiences are constructed by researchers in their interpretations of the interpretations of others, as presented in their written social texts. The implications of this shift from discovery or finding to constructing or making remain somewhat unclear.

However, what it does not mean is abandoning realist uses of photography and video. For example, in the late 1990s I conducted a childhood ethnography in two schools within an Indian district (Chawla-Duggan 2007). I was interested in producing detailed understanding about eight Indian children's school and home lives, and how their social practices which occurred within family life, within friendships with other children and through relationships with teachers, influenced how they approached learning in formal schooling. As part of the childhood ethnography, I used video film and photographs, drawing on participant-generated photographs to conduct photographic interviews with the children, by using the now well-known practice of photo elicitation (see Figures 2.1–2.20), but also selecting my own researcher generated photographs systematically recorded, for illustrations of regular patterns of interaction in school and classroom settings. In this way I was making and eliciting knowledge through discussions about the photographs and illustrating knowledge about children's everyday lives through the photographs, collected as a systematic process. The following photographs are a selection of both the participant generated and researcher generated constructed to illustrate one child's story, Saraswati:

Figure 2.1 Saraswati.   *Figure 2.2* School.

(*Continued*)

Visual technology for educational ethnography 23

Figure 2.3 School playground.

Figure 2.4 Hometime.

Figures 2.5–2.10 Saraswati: Formal schooling and social practices inside the school and classroom

Figure 2.5 Reading to the class: Saraswati reading to the class and madam. She is reading a lesson from the social studies textbook and the class and madam listen as they follow it from their own textbooks.

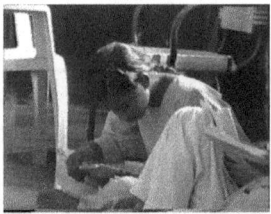

Figure 2.6 Revising Hindi: Saraswati revising her Hindi lesson on her own from her textbook.

Figure 2.7 Revising with peers: Hansa tests Saraswati's Hindi.

Figure 2.8 Solving a maths problem with class peers: Saraswati sitting with a group of girls trying to solve a maths problem. Renu is pointing to the blackboard and the steps madam has written down, whilst Santoshi, sitting next to her, listens.

(*Continued*)

Figures 2.5–2.10 Saraswati: Formal schooling and social practices inside the school and classroom

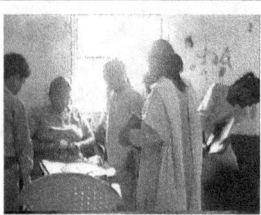

Figure 2.9 Getting maths marked: Saraswati standing next to madam is having the sum on her slate checked. Other children are standing around her, waiting for their sum to be checked too.

Figure 2.10a Being class monitor. As class monitor Saraswati is taking the lesson. She is holding the textbook and asking the class questions from it. Individual children are raising their hands to answer the question. Renu is standing at the side, following the lesson whilst reading her textbook.

Figure 2.10b Being class monitor. As class monitor Saraswati patrols the class and approaches Renu to check her sum. Saraswati is marking Renu's slate and correcting her sum.

(*Continued*)

Figures 2.5–2.10 Saraswati: Formal schooling and social practices inside the school and classroom

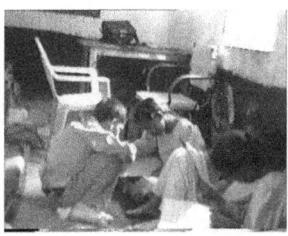

Figure 2.10c Being class monitor. As class monitor Saraswati is answering a query from Pravin about the lesson they are learning from in the Hindi chapter.

Figure 2.10d Being class monitor. As class monitor Saraswati approaches Deepak to show him how and which questions to do in the Hindi chapter. Suresh is leaning over to see how and what is to be done too.

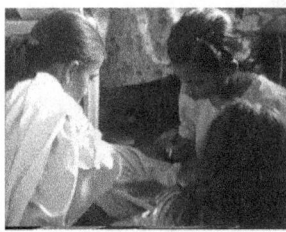

Figure 2.10e (Right) Being class monitor. As class monitor, Saraswati is approached by Pinky to check her sum. Saraswati is marking her slate for her.

Figures 2.11–2.15 Saraswati – Non-formal social practices inside the school and classroom

Figure 2.11 Eating lunch with school friends. Saraswati sitting in the classroom with Santoshi and Leena having their lunch together.

Figure 2.12 Eating an ice lolly with a school friend. Saraswati eating an ice lolly outside the school gates with Minakshi at lunchtime. The ice lolly vendor's bicycle is standing behind her.

(a)   (b)

Figures 2.13(a and b) Buying and eating a snack with a school friend. Saraswati buying and eating a plate of 'gol guppe' (savoury puffs filled with chickpeas and tamarind water) with her friend Minakshi, at lunchtime outside the school gates. The vendor from whom they have bought them sells a plate of 4.

Figure 2.14 Playing games with friends at lunchtime Saraswati plays a clapping and singing game in the classroom at lunchtime with Santoshi and her sister Shabana. Pravin walks in and watches them.

Figure 2.15 Organising a lunchtime game. It is too hot to play outside at lunchtime, so Saraswati is organising a game inside the class to play together. Some of the boys join in too. Renu is standing at the side giving the same instructions as Saraswati. Pravin is standing and watching with two of the girls.

Figures 2.16–2.20 Saraswati – Home social practices outside the school and classroom

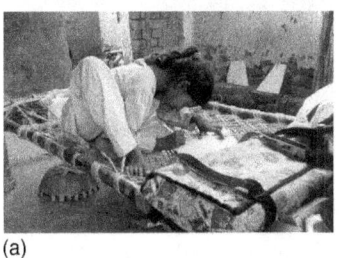 

(a) (b)

Figures 2.16(a and b) Sisters doing homework.

Figure 2.16a Sarasvati: *this is Shabana doing her homework.*

Figure 2.16b Saraswati: *I'm in this one. I'd come home from school and I was doing my schoolwork. These others are neighbours and this is Krishna standing.*

Figures 2.17(a–g) Household jobs

Figure 2.17a Homestead maintenance. Saraswati: *I made this, mum and I (the floor). I've just bathed, that's why my hair is loose. And then I was washing the floor when you arrived. I didn't know how to make this.* RCD: *what did you do then?.* Saraswati: *well at the start it's covered in a white paste. Then you layer it with cow dung and water and leave it to dry.*

Figure 2.17b Fuel for the home. Saraswati (right): *we were just collecting some dung, then Krishna called us.* Shabana: *look I've made all those dung pots.* Saraswati: *well I did, Mona did, and Shabana did. We've put them under there (Saraswati points), so when it's raining, they won't get wet. Right now there's no electricity. It's 12 o'clock and now the light's gone. And at 12 0'clock Shaktiman (Indian superhero) is on TV.*

(*Continued*)

Figure 2.17c Collecting wood for cooking. Saraswati: *this is behind my home, I am cutting wood; she doesn't know how to take the photos, Shabana, I told her when I'm fully in the photo, then take it. I was cutting the wood to take into my house.* RCD: *so do you do this job every day or sometimes?*. Saraswati: *um, sometimes once in two days; sometimes.* Mum: *we have to cut it every day to make the chapattis.* Saraswati: *if its large stick, we just cut them into small pieces and keep them aside.* Mum: *we collect them and keep small pieces in the home to light (in the wood stove).* RCD: *so where do you get the wood?*. Saraswati: *just here, behind us and we collect it from there (pointing to the fields).*

Figure 2.17d Chopping wood for cooking. Saraswati: *here I was cutting it; I was cutting it with an axe; Mona and Meera are sitting behind me; they go to the English school; they're in their dresses.*

(e) (f)

Figure 2.17(e and f) Keeping the homestead clear of animals.

Figure 2.17e Saraswati: *this is just outside where everyone sits in the evening – all the people that live around here. All their children come and we play. We play whatever; but I don't go. That day it was raining, and loads of cows came and I went to move them on.*

Figure 2.17f Shabana: *I was with Saraswati and went to move the cows on. There's a dog there and I'm scared of them.* Saraswati: *because she was bitten before.* Shabana: *he bites everyone around here.*

(*Continued*)

Visual technology for educational ethnography 29

Figure 2.17g Buying groceries with mum. Saraswati: *in this one I (Saraswati is bending over at the front) went to buy vegetables from the market. The market will be on today, in the lane to the plaza. It's the Tuesday market; Many people will go today. This is mum (bending over in the background), this is Krishna (standing), and that little boy Gulu, that's his mum.* RCD: *do you go every Tuesday?* Mum: *yes we go every Tuesday to buy vegetables; its only open once a week.* Saraswati: *Tuesday and Fridays.* Mum: *sometimes we go on Friday, and sometimes Tuesday.*

(a) (b)

Figures 2.18(a and b) Helping in community.

Figure 2.18a Playing with neighbours' children. Saraswati: *this is that little boy that just came. I was playing with him in his house. Sometimes he comes here, sometimes Shabana and I go here.*

Figure 2.18b Child minding neighbours. Saraswati is carrying Gulu, the infant that lives in the homestead across from Saraswati's. Her mother is busy washing clothes and her sister Shabana is watching.

(a) (b)

Figures 2.19(a and b) Playing in community.

Figure 2.19a Playing kites on Kite day. Saraswati: *Krishna is holding a kite; but a boy came and took it. I was rolling up the string of the kite. I was helping that little boy, he lives just here. All these children are from around here. Krishna took the photo. It was kite day.* Saraswati: *all the children play marbles around here. So many people live around here, I can't count them. There are lots of areas for us to play. Over there (behind them) the tank; and some buildings and the Plaza tower. You can see it all. If we go right to the top didi, you can see all the huts.* RCD: *It was up here that you made your dung pats here didn't you?* Shabana: *yes – I did it like this (and Shabana demonstrates the actions with her hands – a bit like the slapping of pizza dough or naan bread).*

Figure 2.19b Playing with the village children. Saraswati: *this is where we play on the rocks; just behind our house. They are all neighbours. They don't go to our school, just one of them – he does (in the brown trousers). They all go to different schools – some to English. 3 of them to there, and 2 of us in Sukunderpur. They're 8, 9 and 10 years old. I was taking the photos. 3 of them are 10 years old. We used to play here (referring to Mona). I used to be madam and she (Mona) used to me my servant, and she used to make my dinner and I used to sit here. She (Mona) used to make my meal and bring it to me.* Mona: *she (Saraswati) used to sit here from the start, and I used to – see these flowers and this grass – I used to drive her car here.* Saraswati: *and then I'd come, and she used to make my meal and leave it here – Mona did (they all laugh).*

Visual technology for educational ethnography 31

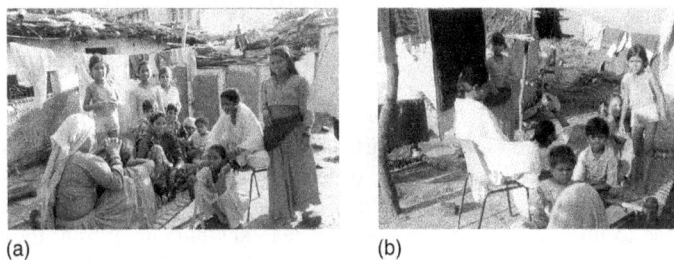

(a) (b)

Figures 2.20(a and b) Sitting in community.

Figure 2.20a
Saraswati: *this is my aunty (not real) that woman who's there in the blue sari. When she comes, then all the gossip comes here; she comes sometimes. I was sitting there and listening to their chatting. They were talking – things like, how does the water get here, do they argue around here, these sorts of things.*
RCD: *so where does the water come from*
Saraswati: *from the tank. It's theirs. They made it. Now they've made 6 taps – it's a big tank. It's made of stone (adds Krishna)*
RCD: *meaning?*
Saraswati: *there's just one tank. On it are numbers are written – no. 1, no. 2 like that. There's a supply of water that comes to the tank through pipes at 5 0'clock every day, and in the morning at 7 0'clock*
RCD: *how do you know?*
Saraswati: *I know the times that the water arrives. Then we go and collect the water in the buckets. We get 2 small, 2 big, and 4 of those that we can carry in other containers. So we get 6 to 8. And we keep them in the bathroom and outside the house.* RCD: *and who are all these other ladies – like the one in the white on the chair?*
Saraswati: *that's my mum.*
Mum: *this is her mum (the sublessees mother), this is her daughter and her son; and there's a mother and daughter who live nearby and there's Shabana. They're all the neighbours. That fat girl was just standing here, she is with them. That's me – that day I wore a suit; my older daughter was leaving that day, so I wore a suit that I was keeping*
RCD: *so you were all sitting together chatting?*
Mum: *yes we all sit together with the children, and Saraswati said 'Mum I want to take a photo'. This woman is 'my mother' (says another woman standing there)*
Saraswati: *it's her mum, the people, who own all this, and her mum was there.*

Figure 2.20b
Saraswati: *this is also that, this has got fewer people in. That's Shabana; mum was tying her plait, with the ribbon*
RCD: *she's making her hair; what time was this then?*
Saraswati: *it was about 4 0'clock at the time; her hair had come open so mum remade it.*
RCD: *so where was your brother Krishna?*
Saraswati: *Krishna was playing there. That family has a little brother, so they were playing.*
....

The images were useful (though inevitably subjective) records of how school and home life happened for Saraswati with visual and material detail found in the home and school context and its activities. The photographic skills of Saraswati (and her sister Shabana), migrant schedule caste, 9- and 10-year-old sisters who lived in a community of 'juggis' (houses constructed from materials of mud and sheets of iron) represented their home culture as a way of life. Yes, the photographs do demonstrate how they participate in constructing a version of their home life for me to understand; but this does not take anything away from their authenticity. The participant generated photographs subjectively framed selected images of Saraswati's everyday life. I used them to structure her experience of everyday home life, and as such part of her home culture. They represented the visible influence of her mother in her everyday lives, a strong sense of having responsibilities, friendships and being part of a community. Drawing on the data analysis from the school environment, I also systematically collected photographs of her everyday school life, and then discussed and selected researcher-generated school photographs with Saraswati to illustrate patterns of interaction. They illustrated a strong sense of responsibility as a class monitor, a participating member of the school community and her friendships. In that respect the photographs and the story they tell about Saraswati were constructed through a collaborative process, using both the participant- and researcher-generated photographs, with which she agreed, rather than a means of objectively documenting reality. Whether the reality varies depending on who is viewing it, is open to debate, as Pink stated:

> Realist uses of visual images in research are not absolutely incompatible with approaches that recognise the contingency of visual meanings. Nevertheless, it is important to keep in mind that even the reality the researcher him or herself sees in the image is framed by her or his own culturally and individually specific subjectivity.
>
> (2007: 124)

The kinds of issues which make contingent the meaning of what's going on in the image can be examined through considering another perspective in visual ethnography, the reflexive perspective.

The reflexive, visual ambiguity and new routes to ethnographic knowledge

Taking the example of video, a reflexive approach to using video involves situating video footage critically in the research process. Being reflexive enables researchers to understand how knowledge is produced through the visual in video recordings, exploring for instance: relationships between the video making device, the video recordings, the person(s) making and analysing the recording, alongside other verbal, written or photographic knowledge produced during the research. A scientific realist and a reflexive approach to the visual therefore differ, in their assumptions about visual representations.

First, a reflexive position assumes it is impossible to photograph or video an objective visual record of any process, event or activity. Second, rather than regulate visual content, when a researcher or participant produces images, they are analysed reflexively, so the informant's subjectivity and intention informs the visual content. Finally, when analysing video or photographs reflexively, its analysis is not only about the content of images but includes the idea of ethnography as a reflexive and experiential process through which our understanding, knowing and knowledge are produced. Accordingly, I maintain it is necessary though insufficient to look at choices made in collecting and analysing visual material; an additional requirement is to ask the reflexive question 'how do we make those choices, and how do they influence the data we get?' This constitutes a reflexive approach to the production of ethnographic knowledge, a process which critically produces an ethnographic portrait of the phenomena under study.

Reflexivity is a responsive theme in visual methods literature, advocated in several texts containing reflections on visual methods in visual anthropology (Banks and Zeitlyn 2015; Rose 2016) and visual sociology (Knowles and Sweetman 2004; Pole 2004; Rose 2013). Such texts represent a time of methodological reflection and a deconstruction of visual methods and visual ethnographies, informed by the postmodern critique of the 1980s (the fifth moment, which may tend to see ethnographies as subjective 'fictions').

My own understanding of reflexivity in this text aligns with the work of authors who challenge the kind of naïve empiricism that tends to characterise the visual as an objective means of representation (Banks 2001; Pink 2013/2021). Added to the challenge, I maintain and have found from my own research experience that it is important to ask reflexive questions, about 're-presentation', rather than 'representation'. From this re-framing, researchers can immediately grasp the idea of visual representations as always constructed, and therefore, are not a means of objectively documenting reality. This 'post-modern like' deconstruction is an epistemological position which underpins a reflexive understanding of visual representations. Whilst those researchers taking a scientific realist position effectively reject a potential in the visual to construct and represent new types of ethnographic knowledge, the reflexive position conversely moves away from traditional ideas of knowledge production associated with scientific realism. For an ethnographer using visual methods, a reflexive analysis therefore means:

> ...considering how ethnographers play their roles as photographers in particular cultural settings, how they frame particular images, what is behind, above and below those frames, and how these choices are related to the expectations of academic disciplines and institutions and those of participants, their visual cultures and relationships, and the politics and power relations of the situations in which we photograph.
>
> (Pink 2021:84)

Certainly, there were politics and power relations at work in my photographs and video filming of Saraswati's school situation. For example, the class teacher told me not to take photographs which included the teacher sitting down, whilst her leg was fractured, in plaster, and rested on the chair. This was because she feared anyone seeing the photographs might assume she was not working and may see her in an unfavourable light, as a government schoolteacher. At one point she also asked me to stop video recording, once again for fear of backlash and critical comments about government schoolteachers. I stopped videoing at that point, as participants in my study had the right to withdraw, and I also did not want to lose her fieldwork support. The example illustrates how politics and power intersect with visual data collection methods, but also ethics, because of the problem of visual ambiguity. On the one hand, as a British researcher, I did not see the taking of photographs and film in this situation as problematic; in fact, it could be commended that, despite being injured, the teacher still attended her work. However, as a person from a traditional Indian family, a reflexive way of knowing the Indian teacher's perspective, in relation to being seen by outsiders, combined with knowing about the significance and value of the Hindi phrase *'log kya kahenge'* in Indian society, led me to understand her fear more accurately. In English the phrase translates as 'what will people say?' and is often used to express fear of being judged or criticised by others in Indian society. For outsiders viewing the photographs, there would be the fear of criticism about government teachers in Indian society, creating harm to their personal and professional dignity.

From a social science perspective, the problem of visual ambiguity is debated through discussions about ways of knowing using the visual. Wagner (2001), for example, suggested that those critical of a 'realist' approach to image-based fieldwork see its advocates (for example, Collier and Collier [1986]; Collier [1967] and Prosser [1998]) as limited in their appreciation of visual materials. But from Pink's (2007) standpoint, using photography and video recording solely to 'collect data' overlooks the value of visual ambiguity. Instead, she maintained the importance of a reflexive position; assuming and believing it to be one way to new ways of knowing and to exploring and reflecting on new routes to knowledge. To add to existing complexity, the additional consideration of current visual cultures represents a broader understanding of conditions producing and negotiating visual representations. It is especially relevant to advances made in digital photography, which acknowledges how:

> ...everyday visual cultures and the practices associated with them are shifting with the widespread photographic documentation and representation of everyday life through smartphone photography, uploading to social media platforms and the rise of the selfie.
>
> (Pargana Mota 2016 cited in Pink 2021: 30)

In practice I would say, reflexivity becomes an even more difficult task with the advent of social media platforms. We live in a time where our understanding of the visual in research also includes understanding how people come to know through the visual; because as researchers, we no longer solely collect visual content as a route to ethnographic knowledge. If reflexivity in the visual depends on a researcher's ability to make sense of the interface between human beings, images, the technology used and our everyday visual cultures, then the kinds of reflexive questions we ask in relation to new routes of knowledge surely pivot on key ideas about everyday practices in which we now make, watch and circulate images, and subsequently come to know and produce knowledge through the visual.

The notion of reflexivity therefore recognises the subjectivity of researchers and/or participants who are 'producers' in representation of ethnographic portraits, but alongside this, also sits the visual cultures we are part of, as we come to know the world. From this epistemological position, subjectivity and the visual cultures we are part of are central to ethnographic knowledge production, interpretation and representation.

Additionally, it is important researchers take account of the visual technologies we use in ethnographic work as part of knowing about human experience and the process of producing ethnographic knowledge. In the following example I present a reflexive approach to using body-mounted cameras to produce ethnographic knowledge. I asked young children to wear body-mounted cameras (GoPro cameras) on a harness as part of a study about how young children experience father–child relationships and its relationship to teachers' perspectives of father's involvement in formal schooling in England. The family included the father Steve, his wife and three children, Ellie (age 7) and twins Michael and Rosie (age 4). They lived in a small rural middle-class village in the southwest of England.

The scene depicted in the following paragraphs is created through Steve and his three children taking a walk in a woodland, close to their home. It is a dreary but dry Sunday afternoon in December. To record the scene Ellie wears a body-mounted camera (a 'GoPro') in a harness strapped to the front of her chest. The following is my fieldwork narrative recording and transcript of the scene, as I watched the digitally recorded video film of it after the event had occurred:

> The three children run across a field, the twins are visible and I can hear the sound of Ellie's breathing as she runs. The three run uphill towards a solitary Oak tree standing in the centre of a wide-open space in the field.
> Ellie watches the twins as they run towards her and the tree. She sees Rosie look around and Michael join her; the twins walk and then run further across the field together.
> No one speaks...there's just the sound of children's rapid breathing. Ellie screams ...
> 'you better move... Rosie you better move', she shouts.
> Ellie looks at her hands wrapped around a pale blue rope, which hangs and swings from the tree; it makes a creaking sound as it moves. She looks down at the bottom of the rope; it's tied to a rubber car tyre. It's a makeshift swing in the middle of the field and Ellie's standing on it.
> '...Michael move...' pleads Ellie anxiously as she swings moving forward, facing fields, then sideways to the left, to the right, backwards, forwards, and backwards again, her breathing getting louder as it keeps up with the pace of movement on the swing.
> 'I can see another field from here...' she shouts excitedly as she moves repeatedly in different directions on the swing, now spinning 360 degrees, backwards, forwards...to me it feels like she's on a fairground ride.
> ....No-one speaks
> In the distance she watches two colored dots; it's the twins again in their respective blue and bright pink coats, running across the field. She looks at her Father watching her as he stands close to the tree's branches; and she swings on the tyre, flying higher now, looking at the treetops.
> Ellie watches her father walk towards her...
> 'Watch this daddy...' she shouts
> 'Not so high...' she screams as she swings high
> She's spinning 360 degrees now, three times, then backwards, forwards ...looking up at a bright blue sky, swinging close to bare branches towering above her. I feel sick and dizzy watching the footage.
> 'not so high ...' she shouts
> 'stop ...no ...stop...she creams...' She spins four times...laughing her head off, swinging and spinning ....

'no...'...

'stop it...stop it...' she screeches

A few minutes later Ellie's pace has changed. Now she's walking slowly, and she's looking down at a stream, watching water moving over rocks, hearing ripples and in the distance, the sound of her siblings' screaming with excitement. Ellie looks up. She watches the twins from a distance, she watches them walk across the bridge above the stream she's been looking into.

...No one speaks.

(Footage transcript: *Comfortable silence: The Woodland Walk*; extracted from – transcript of body-mounted camera footage: GoPro observations)

Figures 2.21–2.24 Scene: Comfortable silence: The Woodland Walk – Video scene extracted from body camera recording)

 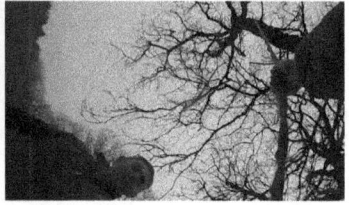

Figure 2.21 'I can see another field guys' shouts Ellie.

Figure 2.22 'not so high ...' she shouts. 'stop ...no ...stop...she creams...' as she spins 4 times...She laughs, swinging through the air.

Figure 2.23 'stop ...no ...stop...she creams...' as she spins 4 times...She laughs, swinging through the air.

Figure 2.24 Crossing the bridge.

Figures 2.21–2.24 represent the transcript and images from the scene recorded by Ellie's body-mounted (GoPro) camera. Figures 2.25 and 2.26 represent images of the children at home and their teachers at school, reflecting on the Woodland Walk scene, presented to them by the researcher. In Figure 2.25 we used video to collect data about children's recollections as a collective endeavour, whereas in Figure 2.26 we used video to help children reflect as they recalled the scene. Through combining video modalities (extraction and reflection) with body camera technology, as an approach to data collection, we collected multiple layers or interpretations of the same scene, constructed through different perspectives, my own as a researcher.

Figure 2.25 Woodland Walk, Scene: Children watching video to recall (video for recall).

Figure 2.26 Woodland Walk, Scene: Teachers watching video to reflect (video for reflection).

The following is a transcript illustrating several issues raised during the teachers' reflections as they watched the video footage of their pupils on *The Woodland Walk*:

T1: They are exploring and investigating, aren't they?
T2: There's none of 'don't do this' or 'don't do that'
T1: He's actually stepping back and letting them go, he's not trying to lead them in anything. He's going in their direction, just following two paces behind. In a way, he's letting them go forwards, but not in a way that is disinterested, he's allowing them and enjoying watching them explore
T2: ... There is no, like, from daddy, 'be careful with that bridge!'... he's just letting them take the risks
    ...He's giving them free rein, really, isn't he? He seems far more comfortable in that environment... Far more relaxed (*than reading to them*), letting them go, and explore, and investigate. Not a lot of conversation
T1: No... but comfortable silence
T2: I think the children... he was allowing them to just go and be children

T1: Discover and explore, the characteristics of effective learning!
T2: ….there's a lot of love there…
(Film Elicitation interview 1 with practitioners: *Not a lot of conversation: Woodland Walk with Father*)

For me, as a previous pre-prep, primary and middle school teacher, I could recognise 'curriculum language' relevant to the content and learning of formal school curriculum in teachers' reflections of the 'The Woodland Walk'; and as an academic researcher I could also recognise possible questions related to pedagogic relationships. For example, teachers used expressive terms to describe a nurturing and (non)regulatory side they saw in the context of this pedagogic relationship, when watching the Woodland Walk scene; terms which are not entirely tangible but through the sensory experience of watching the video scene triggered affective or emotional responses in the viewer about the viewed. In this respect, as a reflexive process of interpretation, their comments tell us more about what the teachers value as noticeable. My own researcher reflexive interpretation of watching (as opposed to listening to) the footage suggested I noticed physical triggers the footage evoked in me. That is, I felt dizzy and nauseous when watching the footage. At certain moments I felt like I was moving in three-dimensional space; in other parts of the footage, I felt speed; the speed at which young children move, that is, the pace of young children's movement, as they ran. I had forgotten how different the speed of their world is, in comparison to the adult world. It was as though I had captured knowledge about her embodied experience (Bates 2013) of moving through her environment, using this kind of visual technology.

There are several reasons for presenting the images from the Woodland Walk scene and my associated reflections. First, it is to demonstrate how different kinds of technology produce different kinds of knowledge. The scene and images represented in no way give you as the reader the sensory experience and affective knowledge viewers (the children, teachers or project researchers) may have felt when watching the scene. Viewers were left understanding a child's (Ellie's) experiences of the Woodland Walk in a different way to readers. This is what Henley (2007) calls a revelatory dimension of filmmaking, unachievable through non-visual research methods. In fact, one of the greatest advantages film has over the literary account, is its capacity to facilitate an empathic understanding on the part of the viewer. Second, whilst that might be one of the functions of film generally, body-mounted cameras in particular (GoPro camera technology) used in this data collection, had the added advantage of providing a further insight into childhood experience. In filmmaking terminology the footage from the body-mounted GoPro camera as a source of data gave a different 'point of view[1]' and knowledge about the child's (Ellie's) experiences. By extension (and third) the 'affect on the viewer' is different to one where the point of view is the outsider looking in (where someone points the camera choosing to film the scene). This in turn elicits '…the most profound type of knowledge [which] is not spoken of at all and thus inaccessible to ethnographic observation or interview' (Bendix 2000, cited in Pink 2015: 5). This means as a childhood researcher I became open to the possibility of another route to knowing children's experiences, from which I could reflect and explore several potential research questions in the study.

Whilst a reflexive position towards using the visual in ethnography hold possibilities for new ways of understanding and knowing social, affective and educational worlds, a third philosophical position from which to look at the relationship between representations of truth and how we get to know that truth is the dialectic. Dialectics here is used in the sense of both identifying contradictions and concretely resolving them, in which the visual is used to capture dynamics of change.

Capturing the dialectic in visual contexts and ethnographic knowledge

The dialectic tradition used here concerns itself with facing and resolving contradictions. In contemporary educational research it is linked with human development, for example, in studies about professional collaborative learning and development or human and child development (see Engeström 1996a, 1996b; Fleer and Ridgway 2014). The roots of dialectic in western social and political thought are often cited with reference to Hegel (1969, 1977) and Marx (1973). To consider dialectic logic in the Hegelian or Marxian sense is to be interested in identifying contradictions and concretely resolving them. One difference between the two theorists lies in what propels the contradiction. For Hegel the source propelling the development of consciousness is their human *Geist* (translated by some as 'Spirit', by others as 'Mind') as they evolve as humans in societies over time. The conflicts lie within the movement of thinking itself and the individual in relation to cultural/societal demands. For Marx, the source of the propulsion is economic forces, of opposing economic groups, of different classes, and the conflict is created by any economic group exploiting or oppressing another economic group (for further discussion of dialectics as a crucial way of thinking and different philosophies of Hegel and Marx, see Langemeye and Roth 2006).

In contemporary applications of dialectical theory, Rainio and Hilppö (2017) draw on the notion of 'relational dialectics' (Baxter and Montgomery 1996). Relational dialectics can be described as ontological dialects, within which reality is understood as fundamentally consisting of opposing forces and their dynamics (Rainio and Hilppö 2017: 79).

Visual technology for educational ethnography 41

Rainio and Hilppö (2017) also see the principle of holism as a common aim in both dialectics and ethnography:

> As ethnography, dialectics also aspires to approach phenomena holistically. In dialectics, this holism...refers to the idea that phenomena in the world are always constituted in relation to other phenomena. From a dialectic perspective, phenomena ...are not dependent as such, nor pre-exist their relations...what sets dialectics apart from other perspectives ...is its focus on contradictions as a unit of analysis.
>
> (79)

From this perspective contradictions as a unit of analysis means the dynamic interplay between unified oppositions (Baxter and Montgomery 1996: 8) where oppositions are part and parcel of the same unified phenomenon (Rainio and Hilppö 2017: 80). For example, we can take individual autonomy and interpersonal relationships as both oppositional aspects of personal relationships. In a personal relationship I am both individually (intrapersonal) and interpersonally oriented at the same time. This is a contradictory social situation. To add to the complexity, Rainio and Hilppö (2017) also argued that, from a dialectical perspective, phenomena in the social world is never defined by one oppositional binary. It is far more complex. Instead phenomena can 'consist of many different oppositional pairs'. For example, enactment – imagined, dependence – separation, mastery – submission are all oppositional elements of agency, and in that respect, dialectics can be defined as oppositions occurring in accordance with 'a driving force through which the phenomenon is in continual movement' (ibid.: 80). In praxis, this interplay is shown through tensions participants feel and encounter. For the ethnographer, it is how people struggle, with or manage those tensions in their actions and interactions that matters. In dialectics, successfully mastering contradictions is seen as the seed of development and therefore change. Here change is not about teleological or predictable change, but movement between stability and change in praxis (c.f. Baxter and Montgomery 1996 cited in Rainio and Hilppö 2017: 80). The movement is continuous in that whilst dialectic contradictions might be mastered, it is momentary and as such a micro transition, through which contradictions emerge again, again and again, as new challenges emerge in praxis.

Using a dialectical epistemological position to study change is not a new idea in educational ethnography. Riegel (1979), for example, saw a dialectic association with knowing about human development. For him human development consisted of short-term situational changes, long-term developmental changes, and their interaction. For Riegel, development (as change) is the result of synchronisation progressions along four interdependent, but unique, dimensions:

1 Inner biological
2 Individual psychological
3 Cultural-sociological and
4 Outer physical

Riegel (1973) also claimed a dialectic perspective could offer useful guidelines for formulating substantive research questions and generating scope and a structure for theoretical concepts relevant to studying educational settings. I would say ethnography (as a method of inquiry from socio-cultural anthropology) provides a compatible set of principles for conducting educational research on topics of interest to dialecticians. In Riegel's dialectical framework (1979) he claimed students could learn ethnographically and think dialectically. This is an interesting proposition, if one considers dialectical interactions between the changing individual and the changing world in relation to how we come to know through visual cultures, as we make, watch and circulate through social media and emerging visual technologies.

Visual technology in and for education is an area ripe for applying dialectics. If we assume one of the purposes of being educated proposed by the philosopher R.S. Peters (1966) remains a commitment to the maxim that it is valuable in itself, then we could argue, in order to achieve what is valued in contemporary global society, education also has the purpose of developing and enhancing the capability of persons within existing social, structural and material conditions. By extension, within the dialectical orientation, visual technology (any visual technology existing materially in educational environments) could be seen as an intermediary, mediating between a pupil, school and society. To accomplish their objectives, teachers and learners can engage in encounters with visual technology inducing dialectical thinking for education. For educational researchers employing a dialectical orientation to study human interaction about education, it is possible to use visual technology such as video in relation to ethnographic-oriented methods (see Chapters 4 and 5). In this respect, there is compatibility between ethnography and dialectics in that there are characteristics in ethnography which correspond to assumptions associated with the dialectic as an ontological and epistemological position. Accordingly, there are possibilities for their combined use in educational research.

In contemporary studies of human development from a cultural-historical perspective, post-developmental methodologies use video and a dialectical model of change (Fleer 2014a). From a cultural-historical perspective, no one part of a system is studied independently of the whole system of interaction. This is an outcome rooted in ideas about dialectal relationships from both Hegel and Marx. But the way contradictions emerge in different pedagogical and educational situations and how teachers, parents or children handle those contradictions in everyday life would be the focus of dialectically oriented studies in education. A few social science researchers working in the field of education and a cultural-historical perspective use the dialectic perspective through studying interactions between teachers and pupils, or pupils with pupils (Rainio 2010; Rainio and Hilppö 2017) and parents and professionals (see, for example, Hopwood and Gottschalk 2017). Such studies provide a deeper qualitative understanding about human development as change seen through interacting human beings.

When considering a relationship between dialectic and development as change (whilst upholding the principle of holism/non-dualism and unity as a theory of mind), it is helpful to see developmental changes as occurring due to a complex web of forces operating on (and being operated on by) an active individual. The changes represent qualitative synthesis of quantitative inputs and are genuine transformations, yielding different emergent forms (see Chawla-Duggan and Konantambigi 2022). In a sense educational ethnography offers dialects a way of coming to truths through its naturalistic approach, and dialectics offers ethnography a general framework for guiding enquires about educational problems concerned with change (Table 2.1).

Table 2.1 Educational Ethnography and Dialectics for the Purposes of Research in Education

Education and ethnography	Dialectics as an ontological and epistemological position
The educational ethnographer has an interest in cultural change as qualitative change.	Dialectics is interested in discontinuous changes, leading to qualitative changes.
Educational ethnography is process orientated.	Dialectics views the person as being in constant movement and process, equilibrium is momentary.
Educational ethnography views socio-cultural context as crucial.	In dialectics the study of human behaviour considers the social, material and historical conditions of a social situation.
Educational ethnographers provide thick descriptions through labour-intensive and time-consuming work.	Dialectics calls for extensive study to uncover the phenomenon.
Educational ethnographers adopt an insider–outsider perspective.	Dialectics emphasise the interdependence of observing subject in relation to the observed phenomenon, observation and interpretation.
Educational ethnographer and participants are co investigators to understand phenomena.	In dialects the researcher and participants are encouraged to engage in collaborative endeavour for understanding.
Educational ethnographers' ability to act as a native is a way to knowledge acquisition.	In dialectics, a criterion to knowledge acquisition is the praxis it leads to (realising theory at a practical level).

The dialectic, human development and visual technology

Assuming human beings have a reciprocal relationship with their environment, they change it in ways that ultimately change themselves. In this respect development itself lies neither in the individual alone, nor in the social group, but in the dialectical interactions of the two; there is no separation. The individual is viewed systemically, as a web of parts in interaction; so that each part derives its meaning from the whole (cf. Wertsch et al. 1996). Development occurs when there is a lack of co-ordination between two dimensions: the individual and social/material conditions. The contradictory conditions, or 'crisis' (Vygotsky 1998a) are seen as an opportunity for growth. So, for example, instead of looking at a relationship between man/woman and the environment as a dualism, sometimes known as the Cartesian model, 'dialectical logic seeks to bring together binar opposites as a synthesis, where both the general and the particular are both-at-once the same thing – as resolving contradictions' (Fleer 2014a: 8–9).

So, the dialectic view is not about stable traits and balanced equilibrium. Instead, the individual, and the world, is seen as a process, in a ceaseless flux of change. Consequently, development does not proceed in linear steps but in dialectic struggles. At the same time, knowledge influences and is influenced by an individual's activities. The concept of 'praxis' is useful here, being concerned with the codetermined interplay between activity and knowledge (Rappoport 1975). In dialectics the purpose is to accomplice change through praxis[2].

Video makes it possible to examine how change occurs from a dialectic perspective (Fleer 2014b). This is because video can capture the complexity of the dynamics which surround material and social conditions that make up the social situation of a person's development and their individual needs, desires and wants, as part of those conditions. In this respect, video is a way of capturing and knowing how change happens, without being dependent on time, as it can observe and capture the dialectic process. This contemporary use of the dialectic in education and human development draws from a body of literature associated with a cultural-historical psychology of education.

Conclusion

Epistemological questions about knowledge and how to get at knowledge are all questions underpinned by notions of truth about social reality and what we believe reality to be. Accordingly, the chapter examined the relationship between ethnographic knowledge and the visual. I have introduced philosophical positions and their connections with using visual technology to produce ethnographic knowledge; those positions being a scientific realist, a reflexive and a dialectic. Specifically, I introduced three ontological and associated epistemological positions underpinning the use of digital photography and video in social science and educational research. Whether defining the perimeters for a representation of reality, or acknowledging how reality is always constructed and therefore inevitably partial; reflecting upon representations of reality allows researchers to ask themselves what kinds of research questions are possible to ask, and what the potentiality is for producing 're-presentations' of reality, and realities as they emerge through using visual technology, to produce ethnographic knowledge.

Notes

1 'Point of view' (PoV) is a film theory concept in which a point of view shot is a scene showing what a character (the subject) is looking at (represented through the camera).
2 Praxis here refers to the realisation of theory in practical terms.

3 Visual technology and invisible pedagogy

Using film and photography to analyse pedagogic culture

Introduction

Historically in visual research, an orientation towards the study of processes, rather than focusing solely on images, led to researchers using the study of symbols (or semiotics) as an analytic tool to study processes (Chandler cited in Prosser and Loxley 2008). In this chapter I draw on a study which used film and photography to explore symbols (as semiotic means) which make up cultures of pre-school slum settings, when delivering the Integrated Child Development Services (ICDS) in Mumbai, India. Visual data clarifies pre-school culture, because pre-school activities such as its pedagogy do not always look like organised pedagogy, as Bernstein's (1975) term 'invisible pedagogy' implied. When examining constructions of pedagogic practices which lead to learning, Bernstein located the kinds of messages existing in English primary schools in the 1960s by examining 36 photographs in the then-influential Plowden Report. The report represented 1960s' child-centred progressive schooling in England. The point Bernstein (1990/2003) demonstrated was that whilst there may not be an explicitly visible hierarchy between teacher and pupil in the images, there is an implicit one in operation, one which creates the contexts. He described the photographs, commenting...

> ...there are children playing creatively by themselves: individual, productive play. There are pictures of children playing in groups, there are children in the school corridors and in the gardens surrounding the school, but it is difficult to find a teacher.
>
> (Bernstein 2003: 67)

In this sense Bernstein maintained the photographs demonstrated a desired culture of teaching and learning, where the teacher's power acts

Visual technology and invisible pedagogy 47

directly on the context of learning, rather than upon the students themselves. He called this invisible pedagogy. Debates about his conception of invisible pedagogy argued that because the rules and criteria are implicit (invisible), they are unavailable to all pupils and their families in the same way (Moore 2004: 141; see also the work of Morais and Neves 2001); therefore, certain students benefit, whilst for others, inequalities remain reinforced.

In the following more contemporary study of child-centred pedagogy, visual data was a way of knowing about cultures of pre-school slum settings; settings who were delivering the ICDS in a district of Mumbai. The ICDS is one of the world's first and largest flagship child development programmes. Launched by the Government of India in 1975, it was the first country globally, to adopt an integrated approach to child development by delivering a range of healthcare, nutrition and early education services. The services were and are delivered via Anganwadi Centers (AWCs), their goal being to help feed, educate, immunise and care for vulnerable children and their mothers, along with data collection on health and nutrition. A crucial aspect of anganwadi policy addresses Early Education. In the study, I was interested in what issues were arising in the early education aspect of the ICDS. The literature maintained that 'quality' of early education required further work, and the ICDS policy itself highlighted the importance of child-centred learning. Accordingly, I decided to use visual data as a way of gaining an orientation into child-centred learning as it was played out through cultures of pre-school slum settings, delivering the ICDS in Mumbai.

My visual data included digital photographs of blackboards, poster displays and film footage of interaction and activities in six pre-school slum settings delivering the ICDS in Mumbai. The chapter discusses and reflects on the methodology of the project. I discuss the relationship between sampling, collecting and editing visual material which represented the culture of the settings, and also the relationship between the structural analysis of my visual data and how I generated theoretical insights, which informed my narrative accounts of pedagogic cultures. Those theoretical insights were set within a broader policy context of prioritising quality early childhood education globally.

To explore ways in which film and photography might shed light on pedagogic culture, I asked myself the following questions. The questions form the basis of methodological issues I raise in the chapter:

1   How were certain images of ICDS pedagogy chosen and not others?
2   How do the images work in supporting or extending other data related to ICDS pedagogy?
3   What lies beyond the 'frame' of the images of ICDS pedagogy, and of what value is the wider 'frame' to understanding ICDS pedagogy?

4 What theoretical insights do the images of ICDS pedagogy provide into pedagogic cultures, the view of young learners and quality childhood education?

For this project, the films and photographs were mainly taken by myself and a field officer in Mumbai, and in this respect, I refer to the visual material as researcher generated. Through discussing the relationship between the visual material, Bernstein's theory of invisible/visible pedagogy and methodological processes, the chapter reflects upon the affordances of using researcher-generated film and photography to provide insights into pedagogic cultures.

The chapter begins with a theoretical-methodological context and a discussion about exploring pedagogic culture through visual data. I then present the policy context of the study, the visual data and its analysis using Bernsteinian concepts. The final part of the chapter discusses what all this means. I draw upon the idea of pedagogic practice being symbolic of a cultural relay, and I reflect upon how cultural relays reveal assumptions about pedagogic cultures and how we view children as learners. The conclusion considers strengths and limitations of using researcher-generated visual data in the study, and the potential of using video and photography, to function as a way of raising questions about quality education through the study of pedagogic cultures.

Pedagogic cultures through the visual

Both ontological and epistemological theory underpins whichever visual research method researchers choose to use. Unpacking the relations between those philosophical orientations and visual methods involves raising questions about how researchers use images and their processes of creation, to produce truthful knowledge about a phenomenon, based on how they understand reality. In terms of the processes of creation, visual research data can be characterised into two positions: those visuals which are researcher generated and those which are participant generated. Historically, anthropologists and sociologists used the former to document and analyse aspects of social life which occurred independent of whether participants knew about or understood images. In such circumstances, a project's aim may not have specifically been intended to be visual.

In this study, I was interested in representing knowledge about the pre-school component of the ICDS as demonstrated through pedagogic cultures in Mumbai slum settings I visited. To represent the knowledge, I turned to Bernstein. His theory of pedagogic discourse (Bernstein 2003) can be used to generate concepts necessary for understanding how teachers or practitioners interpret and practice learner-centred pedagogy (Nyambe and Wilmot 2008).

Bernstein and pedagogic discourse

Bernstein maintained that pedagogic discourse consists of the relationship between two discourses: a discourse of knowledge and skills of various kinds and their relation to each other, and a discourse of social and moral order (Bernstein 2000: 31–32). He termed the discourse which creates specialised knowledge and skills as an instructional discourse (it relates to questions about how and who selects, sequences, paces and evaluates the knowledge learners acquire). He termed the discourse defining social and moral conduct as regulative (it relates to norms of social conduct and social relationships in society and its institutions). He also maintained that the regulative is a dominant discourse, always embedding the instructional (Bernstein 2003). I think one way of interpreting what this means in educational settings is to picture whatever we teach or learn as always held in a pedagogic relationship (although I don't assume all relationships are necessarily pedagogic). Bernstein also stated how a set of internal rules underpin both instructional and regulative discourses. Discursive rules (meaning the rules of selection, sequencing, pacing and evaluation, with accompanying questions about who decides on what is selected, and how sequencing, pace and assessment of achieving selected knowledge occurs), underpin the instructional discourse, whereas the rules of social and moral order (how relationships are positioned in relation to each other, including hierarchy) underpin the regulative discourse:

> The internal logic of any pedagogic relation consists of hierarchical rules, sequencing rule/pacing rules, criteria rules...the hierarchical rules will be called the *regulative* rules and the other rules of sequence/ pacing criteria will be called instructional or *discursive* rules. The fundamental rule is the regulative one.
> (Bernstein 2003: iv, 66 cited in Moore 2013: 160)

He identified a third set of rules underpinning the two discourses, namely: rules of criteria (evaluation) which define what is regarded as legitimate or illegitimate learning in pedagogic relationships. Bernstein (2003: iv, 63) maintained the inner logic of any pedagogic practice consists of the relationship between these three fundamental rules (the regulative, discursive or instructional and criteria); and all modalities of pedagogic practice are generated from the same set of fundamental rules which vary according to their classification and framing values (Nyambe and Wilmot 2008: 5).

Classification and framing

The principle of classification is concerned with the strength of boundaries or the degree of insulation between categories, for example, between times, between spaces, between discourses, between agents and so on (Bernstein 2000: 6). If we take the category of knowledge, it may be configured quite differently to suit what are believed to be the needs of pre-school children, to when they are older. Strong classification assumes different kinds of knowledge must be kept apart; it refers to a curriculum, for example, that is highly differentiated and separated into traditional subjects (Sadovnik 2001: 3). Weak classification assumes they are brought together. If classification is weak, boundaries between contents are blurred:

> Classification thus refers to the degree of boundary maintenance between contents.
>
> (Bernstein 1975: 88)

Whilst classification as a principle essentially translates into structurally positioning what is 'powerful'; framing translates into 'control'; that which regulates moral and social relations within a context.

According to Bernstein, in any pedagogic relation there will be an acquirer and transmitter. Framing is a concept used to describe relations between 'acquirer' and 'transmitter' (see also Hoadley 2006). It is related to the strength of boundary and 'refers to the locus of control over the interactional and locationary features' (Daniels 1989: 125). In this respect framing can be applied to any encounter considered in terms of relationships, communication and power:

> It can refer to the relations between parents and children, between teachers and pupils and between teachers and parents. Strong framing is where the transmitter has explicit control over the communication; weak framing gives the acquirer more apparent control over the communication.
>
> (Power and Whitty 2008: 4)

It therefore refers to that strength of the boundary between what may be transmitted and what may not be transmitted in the pedagogic relationship (Bernstein 1975: 88):

> Frame refers to the degree of control teacher and pupil possess over the selection, organisation and pacing of the knowledge transmitted and received in the pedagogical relationship.
>
> (Bernstein 1975: 89)

> Where framing is strong, the range of options and freedoms is limited. Where it is weak, more degrees of freedom are available to the participants.
>
> (Atkinson 1985: 135)

Using the visual to extract rules governing pedagogic discourse and their classification and framing relations

In general, where framing is strong there is visible (explicit) pedagogic practice, the rules of instructional and regulative discourse are explicit, and the transmitter has explicit control over the selection, pacing and criteria. Where framing is weak, pedagogic practice is likely to be invisible and the acquirer has more apparent control, the rules of regulative and instructional discourse are implicit and largely unknown to the acquirer. In distinguishing between that which is visible and that which is not, visible pedagogy always emphasises the child's performance; whereas in invisible pedagogy the acquirer fills the space rather than the transmitter (Bernstein 2003: 70–71).

Drawing on the above concepts, I used film and photography to extract the set of internal rules (discursive, hierarchy and criteria) together with their classification and framing relations. I then interpreted those extractions, so they explicitly related to modalities of pedagogic practice generated from the rules and framing values. Based on the analysis, I was able to generate questions about the extent to which the child-centred discourse identified in the policy pedagogy of the ICDS was realised within the pre-school pedagogic practice of Mumbai slum settings I visited. I used researcher-generated visual data to conduct the analysis of pedagogic practice and the implicit view of the learner it represented.

Modalities of pedagogic practice and assumption about the child as learner

> A pedagogic practice can be understood as a relay, a cultural relay: a unique human device for the reproduction and production of culture.
> (Bernstein 2003: 196)

Bernstein (2003) argued how the basis of pedagogic practice which gives rise to modalities is rooted in the kinds of learning theories on which the pedagogic practice is based (2003). For example, he considered Piaget, Freud (neo-Freudian) and Chomsky as structurally similar in how they view children as learners and in turn on which they apply theories of instruction. Their similarities are that:

- most are developmental in the sense that what is acquired has meaning only in relation to a particular stage
- the child is active in his/her own acquisition
- the learning is tacit (an invisible act) so the child cannot be modified by explicit regulation

52 Visual technology and invisible pedagogy

- the institution and cultural biography of the child is omitted, and in that respect, they are a-sociological
- most tend to be critical of the transmitter as an imposer of meaning
- most replace domination by facilitation, imposition by accommodation
- the theories imply implicit hierarchy i.e. rules of conduct.

Drawing upon Bernstein's ideas about social relations which exist in any pedagogic practice, I now examine how I used researcher-generated visual data to gather meanings about modalities of pre-school pedagogic practice and what the analysis represented about the assumptions of young children as learners.

ICDS pedagogy and visual images: sampling, logging, editing

Initiated in 1975, the ICDS was conceptualised in response to India's 1974 National Policy for Children (GoI 2011), which was one of the first countries to propose how focused, child-centred interventions would address the inter-related needs of young children and women from disadvantaged communities. To date the objectives for the ICDS established in the 1970s essentially remain the same (with a later provision for adolescent girls).

A crucial aspect ICDS addresses is Early Childhood Education. Within the ICDS, it is the PSE (pre-school education) component that is central to locating its pedagogic discourse. At the time of the study, the official policy-related text described the function of PSE in the following way:

> Pre-School Education contributes to the universalisation of primary education, by providing to the child the necessary preparation for primary schooling...
>
> (GOI 2011: 26)

The PSE component was also central to locating the criteria used for evaluating a child's performance to judge whether they were ready for school:

> The activities which are undertaken as part of PSE include storytelling, counting numbers, free conversations to speak freely and apply their mind in order to organise small activities, painting, drawing, threading and matching colour related to fine muscle coordination and development, reading simple words, writing alphabets words, distinguish objects, recognise pictures etc. The constitution of the PSE kit may vary within a state/UT keeping in view the specific local needs and resources...
>
> (ibid.)

and the pedagogic discourse associated with this [pre]schooling was 'child centred'.

> Under this, child centred play way activities, which is built on local culture and practices, using local support materials and developed by Anganwadi workers through enrichment training are promoted. It is considered the most joyous daily activity of the ICDS programme, which is visibly sustained for three hours a day...
>
> (ibid.)

Critics of early education provision called the ICDS non-functional and uneven (Gragnolati et al., 2005, Dreze 2006), but at the time of the study there was academic evidence to counteract this position (Dreze 2006; Datta 2005). The use of ICDS services in urban areas such as Mumbai was and continue to be affected by wider private options becoming increasingly available to parents (Datta 2001, 2005); the often unregulated, fee-paying pre-schools, inevitably affected ICDS uptake.

Visual images and ICDS settings

A field research officer, two child development project officers (CDPOs) working on Mumbai's ICDS projects, and two anganwadi supervisors accompanied me on fieldwork. The CDPOs were responsible for projects in two slum areas I visited, and the anganwadi supervisors each monitored the operation of approximately 48 anganwadis.

I visited six anganwadis. The sample represented examples of 'good practice' I was shown when visiting two major slums in Mumbai. They were selected by the CDPOs responsible for those slum areas.

Both the field officer and I sought permission to take photographs and videos from the CDPOs and practitioners. The Indian field officer first sought permission verbally, through the local language Marathi. He explained how I was researching pre-school settings, that the research involved taking visual images of pedagogic practice and the environment; and that the findings and images would be used in presentations and writing about researching quality pre-school education. I followed up his explanation in Hindi, assuring them the photographs and footage would be used for presenting research, and if they did not wish me to use images and footage, then I would not do so. One teacher objected to being filmed and so was not included in the footage. Practitioners gave permission to film the children in their classes. As a result, both myself and the Indian field research officer who accompanied me took photographs and films of interacting practitioners and children within their regular activities, alongside the learning environment within which those interactions occurred.

Combining visual data with other data collection methods and researcher positionality

I observed each of the six anganwadis using field notes, videos and photographs. As a source of visual data, the camera was usually pointed at interactions in classroom situations showing 'receivers' and 'transmitters'. Consequently, in certain shots the camera showed closeup pictures of children interacting individually with a practitioner, interacting in groups and interacting as a class, with the practitioner's position identified within each social situation.

I followed up visual recordings of interactions with eight semi-structured interviews which I conducted in Hindi. The interviews were with the CDPO, the six anganwadi practitioners leading the sessions observed, and two supervisors who together provided their perspective on activities I filmed and photographed. In addition, an Indian field officer provided contextual data about the slum areas we visited and their demographics. Finally, I conducted film and photo elicitation interviews in Hindi with an Indian co-field researcher who was familiar with the settings. The film and photo elicitation interviews allowed me to gather information beyond that available in the frame (Becker 1974) of the images in video film and photographs, and in turn, the kinds of structural issues embedding ICDS provision.

Beyond the institutional level of practice, I conducted two semi-structured interviews in English at the local and national level with key officials associated within the Ministry of Women and Child Development, and discussed my experiences and interpretations with an Indian academic colleague whose expertise was the ICDS.

My own positioning, both personally and professionally as an insider and outsider (McNess, Arthur, and Crossley 2015; Milligan 2014), alongside a rationale focusing on quality education which Indian institutions were also focussing on, all helped to facilitate my interactions with participants and in data collection. The rationale for the research arose from several factors. They included: being involved in an international comparative study on quality education, my expertise in early education and integrated provision, my Hindi language ability and research familiarity with India and its schooling. I had in fact been involved in research-related activities in India for some time, having conducted a four-year ethnographic study of children in primary schools and the influence of their home lives for my doctoral work. I am also a part of the first-generation post-colonial Indian diaspora, born of traditional Indian parentage, where both parents came to the UK as a result of 'partition'. In this respect, I was in a position of having some in-depth knowledge, experience and relationships in the Indian community, whilst also being an outsider. All these factors intersected to form my positioning in the research. Mine was a positioning which enabled me to develop a deeper familiarity and understanding of the ICDS in the Indian context of Mumbai slum settings, as I reflected on the visual data and asked questions to colleagues.

Logging, editing and sampling visual material

I logged all photographs and video films in a chart. Logging involved naming, numbering and cross checking with field notes to ensure each image was logged against a descriptive field note of the same anganwadi. The process of logging involved ascribing a number (most cameras allocate them) in a chart and then a thematic title to indicate the content of the image and language (English/Marathi/Hindi) if it was video footage.

When it came to the video material, I undertook a second step in logging video footage, which involved logging visual and audio separately. I began to organise the film rushes by making a transcript of both audio and video material; I would switch off the audio in order to make explicit any existing differences between what I was seeing and what I was hearing. In other words, my video logging examined the visual and then aural aspects of the video film together and separately. Separating the two aspects of video film enabled me to identify any additional information the images could offer, in relation to the aural when analysing footage.

For the purposes of editing and sampling images, I used a theoretical and purposive sampling strategy from the visual footage. It aimed to identify data demonstrating transmitter–receiver social relations and the direction and position of who was in control over what, in the structure of pedagogic communication. If the footage raised other issues outside of this sampling strategy, I documented them in another folder, so if their relevance came to light through other data collection methods, I could retrieve that footage and reflect on its value. My sample included images of visual displays from blackboards and posters, images of children who were not visible receivers, but visibly engaging with content on their own; peer groups who were visible as receivers; and children in positions where they controlled choices, demonstrated through gesture. In this way I included visual representations which highlighted connections and differences between visual and verbal communication.

Additionally, because the theoretical focus for the analysis used principles of classification and framing, an additional column was later added to my logging chart. I called it 'indications of message code', which I based on a structural analysis of pedagogic communication using Bernstein's concepts. This allowed me to quickly see at a glance what the patterns were in terms of message codes indicators across the six anganwadis.

Combining theory and method

The image analysis first used a structural analysis of pedagogic practice. It adopted an instrument incorporating Bernstein's concepts:

> The instrument includes indicators, in the form of two- and four-degree scales of classification and framing, ranging from very strong to very weak (C+, C−, F++, F+, F−, F−−), for various characteristics of pedagogic practice in the instructional and regulative contexts. The number and type of indicators for each characteristic vary according to the context under analysis. The instructional context includes discursive rules (selection, sequence, pacing, evaluation criteria) and relations (inter- and intra-disciplinary, academic....) between discourses. The regulative context includes hierarchical rules (teacher-student and student-student relations) and relations between spaces (teacher-student space and student-student).
>
> (Barrett 2014: 8–9)

I also included the function of body positioning and body gestures as indicators of pedagogic practice relating to space and sequencing. This is because the activities involved in teaching young children may often include non-verbal communication. Additionally, I segmented the film analysis into the order of sequences occurring as the session progressed.

The internal and external narrative of image analysis and the experiential characteristic of video analysis

I do not claim the visual data collected is objective in any sense, or that the evidence I present has not been sampled for the purposes of analysis. In this respect I respond to the question of why I have certain images and not others; and my response pivots on the kinds of theoretical questions I was aiming to address in order to understand the images.

Whilst my initial analytic focus was on the 'internal narrative' of images, that is, I addressed the question 'what is this image of in terms of structures of pedagogic communication?', I also looked beyond the frame (Becker 1974) to explain the external narrative. The external narrative addressed questions of context gleaned from other data collection methods which included documentary policy, semi-structured interviews and photo and film elicitation interview material. This is because usually it is not possible to explain the external narrative by simply examining the image, but through further research data (for example, interview material). The image and their internal analysis are therefore considered in a network of social relationships, which in turn expands a metaphorical frame (Banks 2007) by including wider understandings of policy, place and time within the anganwadi settings of the Mumbai slums I visited. There is also the question of how the images work and whether they extend or support text. In order to explore this concern, the analysis of image content remained open to categories of meaning which went beyond my initial structural analysis of pedagogic communication. Through that openness I was able to recognise differences between the aural in its relation to the visual within the film data. Having said that, Henley (2010) had argued it is important to be free from the despotism of the eye and think in terms of both the aural and visual, maintaining how sound contributes to the development of 'experience-rich' ethnography. In this respect I recognise my use of video films in the study was not purely a visual medium, because sound affects people (particularly young children) in the situations they are in. Conversely, to use film merely as a means of verbally retelling information, as academics are prone to do because of their text-based background, represents an unimaginative and inefficient use of the medium.

What follows is an examination of the pedagogic discourse represented in the visual data from photographs, film and displays. The visual data includes both practitioner–child communication as well as their relation to the materiality of the anganwadi environment. Through focusing on the visual rather than only emphasising the verbal, I present a broader perspective of what I mean by pedagogic discourse. The visual particularly video film, has great potential in representing immediate context in which speech is taking place (Henley 2010). Indeed because the viewer can 'see' the experience alongside hearing it, video can show how any meaning communicated is endorsed, enhanced, undermined or even ignored by features of the transmitter (pace/speed, accent, tone of voice, hand gestures, facial cues); and all this is accompanied by the circumstances and manner in which the information is received and responded to, by those taking part in the pedagogic communication. Accordingly, I maintain video film as a form of data collection can function to provide a broader perspective of pedagogic discourse in educational settings because of its experiential characteristic.

Visual analysis and pedagogic communication – a structural analysis

Background locations of the anganwadi settings

I visited two slum areas in Mumbai's eastern suburban area: Govandi and Mankhurd. In Govandi I visited a place called Ghatla. At the time of the study this slum pocket was 25 years old, with a population of 4000–5000

58 Visual technology and invisible pedagogy

people, mainly Maharashtrian Hindus. Small-scale services and retailers supported its local economy, providing garage services for autos (three-wheeled taxis), selling car parts and general stores. Many of the slum's working population worked in the local markets as 'kulis' carrying fruit and vegetables for market traders. The working population's average net income at the time was around Rs. 6000–7000/month.

Project 'Govandi' operated in its slum areas of Ghatla and Nimoni Bhag. It aimed to improve the health, nutrition and pre-school education of its slumdwellers with its objectives including targets of 'decreasing school dropout, malnutrition, readiness for school, overall development' (CDPO interview). There were 350 anganwadis in the Govandi project and anganwadis operated with minimum resource allocation.

Mankhurd, a suburb in eastern Mumbai, was made up of two residential areas of which one was a slum (20 years old at the time) and the other had a more organised structure, but was also a low-income neighbourhood. There were 272 anganwadis in Mankhurd and I visited a slum pocket called Shivneri Nagar with a population of 3500 people at the time and known for sanitation problems because of its lack of infrastructure:

> the area has a lack of infrastructure facilities; with a number of problems associated with the availability of clean drinking water. Water is currently provided by tankers brought in. Some of the roads are not concrete. There is an open drainage system... so the guttering is all open, giving rise to risk of water related infections such as diphtheria.
> (Interview: CPDO. Shivneri Nagar, Mankhurd)

The anganwadi settings and visual analysis of pedagogic practice

Anganwadi 1 in Govandi

> The anganwadi occupies a room of approx. 3x3m. When we arrive the anganwadi worker (AWW) and co-worker are saying prayers with the children who are all dressed in pink uniforms. There are between 20–30 children present, who are between the ages of 3–5; but look younger. They do a minute of meditation and yogic exercise as part of their morning routine. There's a black board and displays are on the wall. They sing nursery rhymes; first teacher initiated and then class initiated followed by individual child contributions, initiated by the teacher. All the children clap after each child's presentation. The activity changes. The children are all given small slates and the practitioner tells me that they will now do numbers.
> (Field notes, Anganwadi 1 in Govandi)

Visual technology and invisible pedagogy 59

In scene 1 entitled 'Munni behta' (a Hindi nursery rhyme), two practitioners model what and how the Hindi poem should be recited, with all children following the practitioners' gestures and rhyme. The practitioners as transmitters demonstrate complete control in term of gestures (hand movements), pace, rhythm, tone and sequence. The children as receivers clearly know what they are expected to do and therefore the criteria for performing well. They observe and model as they hear and copy the rhyme in chorus, and the direction of the communication is from the adult to the child. There appears to be strong framing in the interactional/discursive and evaluate context of practice, where the rules of selection, sequencing, pace and criteria by which performance is judged is made explicit by the practitioners for children to realise. The direction is then reversed as two children are asked to recite a rhyme on their own and practitioners share a space with the other children. Children are therefore shown to contribute to the selection of content.

In scene 2 'Tell a story – Marathi', control again begins with the practitioner and this is followed by one child being asked to recite a story. It is unclear as to who selected the story but the child is congratulated at the end, indicating that she realised what was required of her as criteria for performing well. For most of the session the selection, sequencing and pace is controlled by the anganwadi worker and in this respect the instructional or discursive rules are strongly regulated (AWW).

The two scenes from anganwadi 1 suggest that framing is strong generally because the boundary between what might be transmitted is fixed (indicated through the discursive rules of the instructional context). There

Figure 3.1 Anganwadi 1 – Image from Scene 1 – Reciting rhyme: Munni Behta illustrating strong discursive rules.

60 *Visual technology and invisible pedagogy*

Figure 3.2 Anganwadi 1 – Image from Scene 1 – Reciting rhyme illustrating weak classification of space and children's contribution to content selection.

Figure 3.3 Anganwadi 1 – Image from Scene 2 – Tell a story: Marathi.

is some agency on the part of certain pupils and for those children the frame weakens, because they can control the knowledge and its transmission to other children. They can recite a story and a rhyme (that has not been recited in this session). The remaining class does not have choice in what is received.

Visual technology and invisible pedagogy 61

Within this strong framing, the visual data showing learning objects for anganwadi 1 suggests the strength of boundary between curriculum content is strongly classified, in that there are mathematics/numeracy development (numbers on the blackboard and slate activity), language development (rhymes in scene 1) and scientific knowledge (science posters), the first of the two being acquired through the skills of listening to practitioners in the first instance. The strong classification and strongly framed instructional and regulative discourse are signs of a visible pedagogy. The availability of limited space affects its use as a shared space between practitioners and children, and children and their peers, producing a weakened boundary maintenance.

Anganwadi 2 in Govandi

This anganwadi is a similar size room to the last one. Again, there are two practitioners present, the AWW and her assistant, with the AWW being the lead practitioner, leading children's activities. The children are not in uniform this time, but what is striking is how practitioners combine English and Marathi. The rhymes they sing are in English and Marathi/or Hindi as are the displays on the wall – English (mainly), and there are photos of key historical figures representing the nation's politicians. The children do an activity where they name parts of the body in Marathi. I am given a written set menu for the children's food and today the children are to be given 'labsi'. It is made of wheat and sugar and will also be distributed to their homes in tiffins, says the AWW.

(Anganwadi 2: Field notes and interview AWW)

Figure 3.4 Anganwadi 2 – Image of Wall displays illustrating strong classification between subject knowledge.

62 Visual technology and invisible pedagogy

In scene 1 and 2 entitled *'Twinkle, Twinkle'*, from anganwadi 2, the pedagogy is once again strongly framed towards the practitioners and the content is an English language nursery rhyme. Similarly in scene 3 entitled '1, 2, 3, 4', the pedagogy is strongly framed. Practitioners direct, select the content, the pace, when, what and how numbers are said and gestured. This indicates strong framing of discursive rules. All the children observe and model the same content with the same gestures, and in this respect, the realisation of the tasks follow a set order determined by the practitioner. The strength of boundary between content indicates a strong classification: English rhymes and numbers in English. Similarly in scene 4, 'Watch the pointer: A, B, C, D', both the hierarchal relation and discursive rules are strongly framed, as practitioners direct, select the content, the pace, when, what and how alphabetical letters are to be recited and gestured. This once again indicates strong framing of the instructional context and what the children are expected to learn. The evaluation criteria are made explicit as children model exactly what is made public in how they present their responses as directed and determined by the practitioner.

English is a very strong part of what is taught and displayed in anganwadi 2. Whilst the instructions are given in Marathi in all scenes recorded, the content of what is to be learnt is in English. The sequence of communication also implies that the children have always to listen first. Listening therefore becomes an important part of learning skills, and the instructional context in terms of being able to recite what is to be said, its pace and its rhythm, all of which is practitioner directed. The child as a learner

Figure 3.5 Anganwadi 2 – Image from Scene 4 – Watch the pointer.

Visual technology and invisible pedagogy 63

(a)

(b)

Figure 3.6(a and b) Anganwadi 3 – Image from Scene – outside and inside the setting.

seems to be learning how to listen as a learning disposition. A similar pattern arises in Anganwadi 3 where the children are predominantly receivers and adults are transmitters, although there are once again examples where individual children recite to the class, indicating a weakening of framing between child–child relations.

The second area I visited was Mankhurd. I visited three anganwadis in Shivneri Nagar, a slum pocket of Mankhurd. The first one (anganwadi 4) was a rented room in a house, let out to AWW workers for Rs. 500 per month.

Anganwadi 4

> When we arrive at the house the children are singing nursery rhymes and doing the actions of various animals as instructed by the AWW and her assistant.
>
> Researcher: so what's your usual routine?
>
> AWW: well first we sit them down and pray, then we sing songs; we'll do rhymes and actions like being an elephant, being an animal in water; how the animals walk, being a monkey. Then we'll have lunch and we'll end with a prayer. For homework I ask them to practice what we've done and tell mummy what they've done…. The purpose of this is for practice and so they are to tell their mummy about it.
>
> (Interview: AWW; anganwadi 4)

In anganwadi 4, within the scene 'Pretend to be animals – representation, gesture and space', the lead AWW directs two children to represent two animals. The AWW directs the children in terms of which animal, how to portray the animal with their bodies, that is, where their arms should be, whether they should be crawling, and which space should be used.

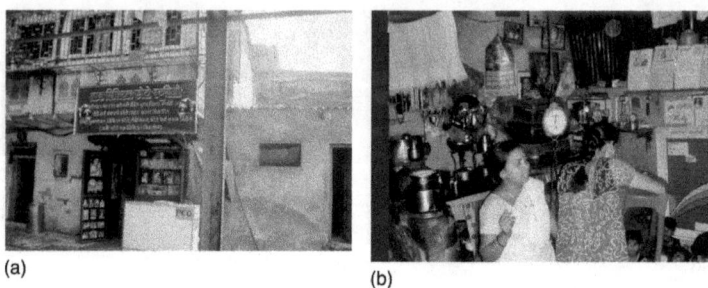

Figure 3.7(a and b) Anganwadi 5 – Image from Scene – outside and inside the setting.

Anganwadi 5

> The fifth anganwadi we visit is a room with a shop at the front of it. It is very 'snug' and the children have to be quite ordered in such a small space in order to take part in the target throwing game they are playing. Nonetheless they are encouraged by the AWW and her assistant to knock over a tower that stands on a stool by throwing a soft ball towards it; even the children who are unsuccessful are encouraged.
>
> (Field notes: Anganwadi 5)

In Anganwadi 5, the scene is entitled 'stacking cups'. It suggests that children are being shown the development of hand–eye co-ordination as a skill. It is not linked to anything else being taught so it is a strong boundary in terms of it being the development of a skill through an enjoyable activity. The transmission is highly regulated in terms of who controls the sequence of how the learning progresses and overwhelmingly in this sequence is a strong framing of an instructional context. The adult selects the child, the adult hands the equipment to the child, the adult prepares the child by standing him/her up. In short, the adult organises who does what and when, that is, the selection and sequence; and the adult initiates the clapping, when the child attempts the requirements of the task (to knock over the stacking cups). The choices transmitted and received for the child are given and there is little room for manoeuvre in terms of what the child is told, and when and where. The only choice seems to be how the ball is thrown as it is not modelled. Having said that, what is interesting to observe is how there is a weakened framing, mainly because the children are actively participating in an activity on an individual basis, which creates a space for more potential interaction between practitioner and individual children.

Visual technology and invisible pedagogy 65

Figure 3.8 Anganwadi 5 – Image from Scene – Stacking cups.

I asked the practitioner (AWW) to tell me more about her work in delivering the education component of ICDS, and her response indicated a strongly integrated approach towards child development, beyond the purely cognitive:

> AWW: ... Today we have been putting in their minds what they should learn before going to school, what is needed before going to school. That's related to their surroundings, the names of the things around them so that they are aware of their environment; poems; how they should wash. The habits are formed ..... If the children don't come here, we go and get them. They don't have the habit so we bring them and we show them the charts (points to fruit and vegetables). We make them aware of the sounds and things around them, the animals and where they live..... I am responsible for about 100 children... They don't eat at set times at home, but they do here and then its gets supplemented at home.
> (Interview with AWW: Anganwadi 5 – Shivneri Nagar)

Anganwadi 6

When we arrive at the last anganwadi, the children are about to eat lunch. The wall displays are of published charts written in Hindi. The practitioner tells me about her routine.

66 Visual technology and invisible pedagogy

Figure 3.9 Anganwadi 6 – Setting up to eat together.

> AWW: We arrive at around 10 am and clean up the place before the children arrive at around 10.30 and we sit them down. We begin with prayers. Then I might ask the children about anything special that's happening at home, or if they're wearing new clothes, whether they are going somewhere special. Then we might do naming of body parts, some nursery rhymes, and words and actions.
>
> (Interview: AWW anganwadi 6, Shivneri Nagar)

The scenes for anganwadi 6 introduce the health component of the ICDS programme where a nutritious food supplement is distributed. Strong framing of the regulative context is demonstrated where adult practitioners control where eating occurs, and the children sit in their spaces, free to decide whether they wish to eat or not.

Generating theoretical insights that inform narrative accounts

The visual analysis of both footage and photographs through a Bernsteinian 'language of description' in all six anganwadis indicated strongly framed discursive rules in terms of selection, sequencing and evaluation of content governing children's performances in the instructional context, accompanied by a strong framing in the regulative context. In this strongly framed regulative context, practitioners were mostly authoritative rather than facilitative. It was accompanied by a strongly framed instructional discourse, to produce a visible pedagogy.

The central point emerging from the theoretical analysis of pedagogic communication through the study of video film and photographs was how the forms of pedagogy I observed did not map onto the espoused 'child centred' pedagogy associated with weakly framed regulative constructs. In this respect, my visual analysis indicated there was a mismatch between the discourse of child centredness promoted in the ICDS documentation and examples of good practice I visited. The mismatch presented an opportunity to ask questions about what is meant by child centredness in different national contexts, so that for participants taking part in those national settings, child-centred pedagogy takes on a more context-oriented meaning. I also maintained the analysis raised questions about capitalising on the scope for more weakly framed relations between practitioner–child and child–child relations within the anganwadi context, and a suggestion for a mixed pedagogic practice of weak and strong classifications and framings. I referred to indigenous models of apprenticeship existing in Indian society with ways of framing which might be helpful when considering a notion of child-centred education, one which is more in line with Indian educational values, adult–child pedagogic relationships in Indian society, and giving voice by acknowledging the beliefs of those participating in the anganwadi settings (the children, families and AWW practitioners):

> ...the true alternative to rote in the Indian context was...apprenticeship...Now this form of pedagogy, and its assumptions about the learner and the learner – teacher relationship, have central place in Indian culture...Although it is predicated on teacher authority, it is not the same as the Brahmanic ashram education that Kumar claims has degenerated into modern day rote learning, for its form on initiation develops skills which can allow the novice eventually to disengage from, and perhaps surpass – rather than merely copy – the expert.
>
> (Alexander 2001: 559)

For Alexander, the apprenticeship approach is a sophisticated counterpart to Bruner's theory of imitative learning, seen in the teaching of classical dance and classical music in India. It combines imitation with dialogue, knowledge transformation and, I would argue, implicated in this, is self-regulation and self-discipline. Accordingly, it may be more easily aligned to a version of child centredness appropriate to an Indian educational context.

Conclusion

Whilst analysis of the substantive area of this chapter was upon the structure of pedagogic relations and how it reveals a message system about pedagogic cultures, the chapter's methodological focus reflects on how I worked with video footage and photographs in the study to gather information about how the educational component of ICDS was interpreted and implemented in a sample of settings demonstrating good practice.

I analysed visual data collected from six anganwadis within two Mumbai slums, using Bernstein's (1971) concepts, associated with social relations in pedagogic practice and communication. At the time of the study I was interested in exploring the kinds of modalities existing in cultures of pedagogic practice operating within Mumbai slum settings delivering the ICDS, and possible assumptions underpinning those modalities, and what this meant in terms of how young children are viewed as learners within a proposed child-centred discourse. My methodological reflections suggest that using researcher-generated visual data from video and photographs, combined with other more traditional methods of data collection, is a way of 'gaining orientation' (Gold 2007) and as such the analysis can inform how researchers identify grounded questions. Visual analysis in this study suggested that my research questions needed to start to take account of how participants arrived at meanings about child-centred pedagogy in those settings and that their national and cultural-historical contexts required addressing; and this occurred as a discovery from the visual analysis.

The visual data used in this study was indeed a way of gaining orientation into the culture of anganwadis in slum areas I visited. Capturing a sense of the 'invisible/visible pedagogy' through examining photographs and videos offers a theoretically informed methodology for other researchers in the field to consider when analysing the structure of pedagogic communication in school and classroom settings. Using a Bernsteinian 'language of description' helped to inform conceptually led questions which were contextually grounded. Bernstein's concept of boundary and related principles of classification and framing provided a framework for exploring the positioning of childhood discourses, and in highlighting how discourse is heard, raising questions for me about how childhood discourses might be recontextualised. In this way I believe longstanding national programmes with strong existing infrastructures like the ICDS might be able to transform opportunities in ways which are more aligned to a version of child centredness appropriate to a range of contemporary and traditional Indian contexts, populations and demographics which exist across the subcontinent.

4 Video modalities as a psychological technique

Studying human development qualitatively and its implications for making learner agency visible

Introduction

Whilst educational researchers have for some time used video in data collection with children (see, for example, Clark 2005, 2007; Thomson 2008) primarily because of its participatory and equalising potential (Pink 2021), rarely do they use it to study human development. The exception to date is the cultural-historical perspective of human development, in which video-based research helps in examining the social basis of the development process (Ridgway et al 2016). This chapter builds on that perspective, by drawing on wider methodological literature from social science, which examines video in research (Haw and Hadfield 2011). I reflect upon a study where I used two video modalities: video for the purposes of extraction and video for reflection. I used two video modalities to shed light on processes of child development occurring through adult–child interactions. In the chapter I focus on child development occurring through father–child interactions in families. One of the unintended consequences of using the two video modalities in my research was how I found they provided another way of using video methodology to uncover ideas about agency. Agency is a complex and debated concept. On the one hand, agency is a process of interaction with material resources, social institutions and the collective efforts of individuals. On the other hand, individual efforts and individuals' understanding of themselves as agentive can be seen as crucial for agency to become possible (Rainio and Hilppö 2017: 83). In the methodology cited in the chapter, the use of video for extraction and video for reflection demonstrates both dimensions of agency in children.

The study was interested in how learning and opportunities for development occur through father–child interactions within family contexts, from the child's perspective. Specifically, the research question was about how opportunities for development are created through father–child relationships in families and the implications of this for a child's development.

DOI: 10.4324/9781003000549-4

This research problem was the impetus for the methodological study. The methodology proposed to use video film to extract examples of dialectic conditions as a way of identifying opportunities for child development. From a cultural-historical perspective of development, this would enable researchers to make visible how the social becomes the individual. Methodologically it meant extracting contradictory conditions associated with the person-social/societal dialectic in the Hegelian sense. In the study the conditions extracted were the child's perspective (motive, more precisely) in relation to demands from his/her social and material conditions of which s/he was part of, in everyday family interactions. One of the unintended consequences of using video for extraction in this way to study human development processes, was how the analysis of conditions within the extracts revealed a deeper understanding of agentive qualities associated with children's learning, which might otherwise have gone unnoticed if the data only examined visible efforts.

The methodology for the study also used video for reflection to gather children's interpretations when tasked with commenting on video extracts. Commenting on video extracts (stimulated recall) in research is nothing new. However, one of the unintended methodological findings from the study was also how using video for reflection with young children can provide insights into the affective and cognitive consequences young children display as a consequence of a 'mirror effect' on themselves. This might be because using video for reflection is both reflexive and dialectic, but clearly it has implications for using video for reflection in studies with young children. It raises questions about how video for reflection may trigger agency that involves ethical considerations for childhood researchers. I discuss the issue later in the chapter.

The chapter is divided into four parts. Part one critically discusses existing constructions of video modalities in social science methodological literature, in the context of research methods used with children. Part two outlines how the research design in the study about fathers and child development planned to use two video modalities: extraction and reflection. In part three, vignettes from the study demonstrate how the research team collected and analysed data in two modalities, identifying methodological issues raised in practice. The concluding part reflects upon the value of both video modalities and practical implications for social science and childhood researchers.

Video modalities in social science research

According to Haw and Hadfield (2011) it is possible to classify video into five modalities in social science research projects: extraction, reflection, provocation, participation and voice. The idea of different modalities is an interesting way of delving into how we use video in social science and educational research, and it enables researchers to critically experiment with using video in different ways.

Video modalities: extraction, reflection, provocation, participation and voice

In its extractive modality, video is a data collection method which functions to extract representation of phenomena. The representations (or video artefacts) are either created by researchers themselves or by participants in the study. Critics of the extractive modality argue it is used to make assertions about intentions and perspectives of participants, when it only actually provides data about 'visible' behaviours (Wagner 2006). In our study we demonstrated how using video for extraction can provide data beyond the visible, and this is because of its link with theory in the research design.

Reflection is a way of using video as a data collection method to present 'objective' images of the participant back to themselves, either self-generated or by others, who hold the mirror up to the observer for a response. Using provocation as a video modality is an extension of a stimulus for reflection. The difference is that the researcher constructs the latter (provocation) of the two modalities to provide a more critical approach, which might challenge ideological perspectives for example. We might therefore assume using video for extraction is a prerequisite to using it for provocation, in that the researcher constructs the extract to provoke in some way. Typically, researchers use video extracts to provoke participants to critically examine and challenge existing norms, traditions and power structures. Tobin et al.'s (2009) seminal 'Pre-School in Three Cultures Study' is an example of this modality. The research team used provocative video extracts from pre-school pedagogy in China, Japan and the USA as cues to stimulate reaction and reflection from teachers, administrators and early childhood education experts, about each other's practice and values underpinning their practices.

Perhaps the most common video modalities for childhood researchers are participation, articulation and voice (Clark 2005, Clark and Moss 2011; Thomson 2008; Lipponen et al., 2016). In these video modalities, researchers often support marginalised members of society who may not be recognised or heard to articulate their voices with the aim of achieving broader social changes. Theoretical traditions about children's rights and the sociology of childhood (Qvortrup 1994; Christensen and James 2008) underpin the use of image-based research more generally through these modalities. Photo voice, frequently used in studies with children is an early example of using photographs and words for modalities of participation and voice, used to empower silent voices to influence policies and programmes (see Wang and Burris 1994 for its early use as a participatory health promotion strategy with women in rural China). The method 'photo voice' has been adapted to different settings and populations and used in conjunction with other visual methods such as collaging, drawing and mapping in participatory studies.

However, uncritically accepting researchers' claims from images or video as a neutral vehicle to access children's participation, voice or perspectives (Buckingham 2009) is a powerful criticism against educational researchers using such modalities. In fact, critics go as far as saying:

> ...those interested in video as a way of negotiating issues of empowerment, enablement and emancipation are constructed as a novelty act, the three 'Es' who lack an in-depth understanding of research and tend to conflate it with creative, political and therapeutic processes.
>
> (Haw and Hadfield 2011: 2)

Lipponen et al. (2016), who are cultural-historical researchers, extend the criticism, arguing it is too simple to say photos mediate children's experiences and offer a window to understanding their perspectives. When referring to voice, researchers are essentially concerned with the extent to which a child is positioned to be agentive. But to what extent can children's views be adequately expressed though the visibility of talk alone? The non-verbal signals of behaviour, clothes, music, apathy, loyalty and silence are all indications of voice and a strong justification for using the visual to represent their position. Central to the video work of cultural-historical researchers Fleer and Ridgway (2014) and Hedegaard and Fleer (2008), is the notion of 'motive' or intention as part of a child's perspective and, more precisely, as a part of their social situation of development. Hedegaard and Fleer (2008) examine child development dialectically to arrive at a child's motive in that situation. Accordingly, video is used to capture dialectic conditions of the child's social situation (Vygotsky 1998a, 1998b). In this study, looking at conditions dialectically shed light on another way to conceptualise agency and the child's agentive perspective, which might have remained uncovered had we not used video for extraction.

The study, video modalities, development and the dialectic

The research team[1] studied 12 families in four countries: England (3), Hong Kong (3), Norway (3) and India (3). The families were heterosexual and middle class, living in the same household with at least two siblings, the youngest being a pre-school child of approximately 4 years old; the oldest having started school and aged between 5 and 7 years. The unit of analysis for the study was children's social situations of development within 'family activity settings',[2] recognised through dialectic conditions created through father–child interactions. We focused and foregrounded one or two children, depending on the activity settings participants filmed. We selected middle-class fathers because middle-class employment can generally accommodate fathers' parenting roles, their employment giving more apparent control over their hours of work. Of course, having some control over employment cannot be considered in isolation; rather, it is part of an explanation which requires understanding how the cultural values of a society play out at institutional levels in families and work, and through the choices fathers make in how they navigate parenting roles at an interpersonal level. For some middle-class fathers that may indeed mean giving more time and availability to the demands for self-employment rather than their parenting role. For others it offers greater opportunities for availability and engagement in their parenting role. In this respect, we considered several factors when analysing the substantive issues of father–child interactions and their relationship to the child's opportunities for development (Chawla-Duggan and Konantambigi 2022).

Data collection

Data sets for the study included:

1 Participant footage.[3] Participants themselves (children or with their parents) chose and recorded up to ten regular activities of father–child interactions.[4]
2 Film elicitation interviews with children/fathers.
3 Film recordings of film elicitation interviews (researcher footage).
4 Semi-structured interviews with fathers.

Overall, we collected up to ten hours of combined participant and researcher-generated footage for each family.

The role of theory

Theory and method were intertwined in the project. Our methodology used two video modalities: extraction and reflection. An extractive modality allowed us to extract social and material conditions of children's social situation of development, to make visible their motive, and identify opportunities for development occurring through the interactions with fathers in family activity settings. As Fleer states:

> Video observations can capture the complexity of the dynamics that surround the material conditions and social expectations that make up the cultural nature of the child's development.
>
> (2014a: 18)

We were able to contain this dynamic by extracting children's social situations of development from video footage of their everyday family interactions with their fathers. This was therefore a naturalistic research design, ethnographic in orientation, and therefore different to how video has been applied in earlier cultural-historical research about learning and development. Additionally using video for extraction to study children's social situation of development allowed us to capture each child's unique context of interaction, giving us indications of their opportunities for development...

> ... through investigations of the qualities of social situations of development they contain. By 'the quality of social situation of development' I mean its developmental potential, i.e. a unique combination of developmental conditions and cultural tools the social situation contains. As such, socio-cultural environments become objects under study not because they influence development but because they contain social situations of development as initial stages of processes of development.
>
> (Veresov 2014: 219–220)

The theoretical and ontological framework associated with the social situation of development are dialectical. Dialectical thinking from a cultural historical perspective is rooted in the work of Hegel (1969, 1977) (see Chapter 2). Rainio and Hilppö (2017) also develop a version of dialectic thinking which they associate with interpersonal relationships and opposing forces:

> ...relational dialectics can be described as ontological dialectics within which reality is understood as fundamentally consisting of opposing forces and their dynamics.
>
> (Rainio and Hilppö 2017:79)

It is the ways in which those opposing forces work in relation to a learner's development, which was of interest to me as an educational researcher. In studying children's development, it is the learner's motive in relation to how they see the social and material conditions demanded of them, which can create opposing forces for the learner. It is the ways in which those opposing forces are handled (by the parent or teacher or peer for that matter) that opportunities for development can be discerned or missed through dialectic movement. Successful mastery of these opposing forces, as contradictions, can be seen as the seed of development and change (see, for example, Engeström 1987 and Chapter 5 on using visual methods in intervention work with practitioners).

The participants themselves created representations of father–child interactions. First, children chose situations in everyday family life in which they interacted with their father. We called these activity settings (Hedegaard 2008). Children then recorded (sometimes with their parents) those situations. Second, we theoretically sampled the footage for children's social situation of development by extracting 'conflict' episodes within activity settings. In other words, the child's behaviour suggested a moment of 'crisis' (c.f. Vygotsky 1998a) in which a possible contradiction existed between a) the child's motive and b) how the child interpreted the father's motive in the activity setting. Through this dialectic framework we aimed to identify and analyse the social and material conditions propelling the child's motive and developmental opportunities. We also sampled footage for children's social situation of development by extracting episodes of emotionally charged behaviour in their interactions, because we assume humans can express conflict through linguistic and non-linguistic ways. In this respect:

> The emotionality of the data can give clues and direction for how the data is to be worked and what might be noteworthy…Emotionality captured as a system of exchanges is made possible through video observation and analysis…
>
> (Fleer 2014a: 27)

We analysed extracts of dialectical situations for key elements of the child's social situation, their associated motive and opportunity for development. We then used the extracts of conflicts for reflection with the children in film elicitation interviews. Figure 4.1 illustrates our methodological framework, what I call the 'Video and Vygotsky' modality.

Ethics

As the lead university researcher, I obtained ethical approval for the project through my own university systems, from overseas collaborating institutions linked to the study, from parents and children, and followed the British Educational Research Association ethical guidelines.[5]

Case study illustrations of extractive and reflective video modalities

The following case study examples first analyse data from an extractive video modality; and second, from a reflective video modality. The analysis sheds light on how the study gathered information about child development through two modalities, whilst also demonstrating learner agency.

76 *Video modalities as a psychological technique*

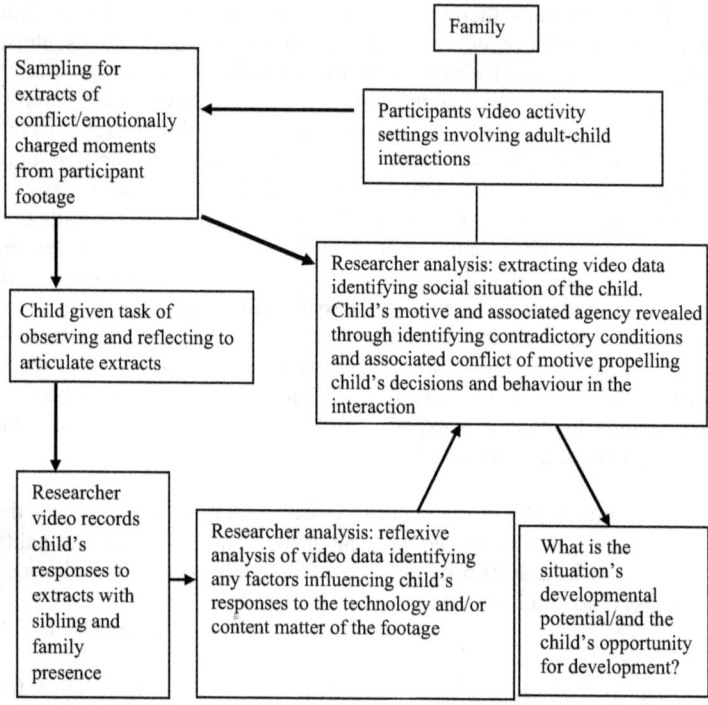

Figure 4.1 Video and Vygotsky Modalities: Video modalities as a psychological technique to study opportunities for development and agency.

Using video for extraction

Case study example 1: Norway – Mr and Mrs Simonson: activity setting – playing games (cards)

>It is a weekend in early November at home. There are two children in the family, Rhoda (aged 6) and Rhandi (aged 4). Rhoda and her father decide to play a game of cards whilst sitting at a small table opposite each other in the living room. Together they create the activity setting of playing games. The mother records the setting by locating a camera on a tripod in the corner of the room. Rhandi, the younger sister, plays on her own but on one occasion steps into the card game to take a card, for which she is rebuffed by her sister. Rhoda and her father speak in Norwegian, but the visual interpretation of the video extract allows some understanding of Rhoda's social situation of development before translation occurs.

At the beginning of the game Father holds his deck of cards and Rhoda's lie on the table next to her. A remaining pile of cards sits in the centre of the table, alongside Father's cup of coffee and a small pile of biscuits which Rhoda eats, in between taking her turns.

In the conflict episode, father puts down a card from his deck onto the pile in the centre. Rhoda looks at it and comments; father responds, to which Rhoda raises her voice in disagreement, then picks up the card her father has just placed into the centre and swiftly hands it back to him. Father takes the card from her, points to the existing card that sits on top of the pile in the centre and returns his card on top of the pile, whilst giving an explanation. At this point Rhoda raises her hands and voice and slaps one hand on the table, all gestures which demonstrate strong disagreement with her father's decision in this game of cards.

In response, her father laughs and continues to explain. She picks up his card from the centre, hands it to him, and places the last of her own cards into the centre. The conflict seems to have been resolved. She puts her elbows on the table, hands wrapped around her chin and cheeks, and smiles at her father, looking as if she is listening to him as he continues to explain and collect the cards together to signify the end of the game.

(Video film observation notes: extracted participant data; Norway Family 1)

Figure 4.2 Norway, Participant footage – Playing games (cards).

In the above video extract, Rhoda is in a situation where she is playing a game of cards with her father and her father is playing by rules. As a result, her motives become conflicted. On the one hand, she wants to play and win, but on the other hand, she knows if she plays by the rules (as her father expects) it will be difficult for her to win. Rhoda decides that, to win, she will change the rules. She then uses this decision to transform the conditions of the game, in that she has a game strategy (to change the rules to her advantage). Her father notices the strategy and prevents her from succeeding. Through his response to the way she plays the game (he creates conditions showing obstacles to what Rhoda wants), we can extrapolate a contradiction between what she wants and what she sees is demanded of her in this interaction with her father. We can trace and make visible not only her motive but the conflict of motives that resulted in her decision and behaviour. We can also discern a higher mental function (developing strategic advantage) and associated opportunity for development afforded through this interaction. In this respect, combining video for extraction with an analysis of the child's social situation of development is a way to allow a researcher '...not only to visualise the process of how the social becomes the individual but to analyse this process in all its dialectical complexity' (Veresov 2014: 224). That is, we can identify the features of Rhoda's social situation but also have an indication of her higher mental functions made visible through how she attempted (albeit unsuccessfully) to transform the conditions of the situation. Her attempts to transform the conditions of her situation also indicate a state of agency.

Later in interview, Rhoda's father explained how he saw his daughter's motive emerging:

Rhoda: Daddy put two cards, but it's not allowed...
Father: the game...has a set of rules, sometimes she, she makes her own rules...And she makes rules that will fit her, so she can win....I tried to explain her that uh, that it wasn't all right to, to decide rules into the game, the rules were set before we started the game... you cannot change that.
(Elicitation interview Father and child: Norway, family 1)

The above example demonstrated how we used video in its extractive modality to collect and analyse data. In the following I demonstrate how we used video in its reflective modality in the study.

Using video for reflection – an example

Case study example: Hong Kong – Mr and Mrs Lam: activity setting, playing games (tennis)

Mr and Mrs Lam in Hong Kong have two children, Anna (aged 7) and Alex (aged 5). Alex is an active child who likes to move about rather than sit still. In the following illustration, Alex is watching an extract of an activity setting created through a game of tennis between Alex and his father. His father is a qualified tennis coach who plays regularly, sometimes coaching his son:

> Alex is sitting with his elder sister Anna, watching the activity setting 'Playing Tennis'. We are in one of his father's teashops. The children

Video modalities as a psychological technique 79

are sitting at a table in front of the laptop computer. Myself and a Cantonese speaking Hong Kong translator (CC), sit beside them. We watch and stop the footage at certain points, when I ask questions to find out what is going on, to understand Alex's social situation. We record the responses and interactions on a digital camera, which is set up in the corner of the shop on a tripod.

(Video film observation notes: Researcher footage – elicitation interview: HK Family 1)

The problem of developing attention

At the outset, it seemed that Alex did not want to give the extract his attention. He was more interested in playing with the video equipment set up in the tea shop to record responses to footage. His motive was evident in his protest, recorded in the researcher footage:

Image/clip time	Non-verbal – observation transcript
Accessing Alex's attention Clip 1: 00:00–1:31  Figure 4.3 Hong Kong, Researcher footage – Video for reflection and accessing children's attention.	In the foreground, Anna (the elder sibling) watches the participant footage and talks about what she sees. Anna speaks in English for much of the time and is therefore able to speak directly to myself. In the background – Alex is trying to set up equipment and look at us through a camera with tripod; his father tries to stop him from fiddling with the equipment and Alex starts to shout; at which point his father lets go and mother steps in. ...In the background a conflict is created through mother and child quarrelling about Alex's attention to the equipment.

In the above scene the research team was expecting Alex to join them to watch the video extract but Alex did not want to give it his attention. He wanted to play with the equipment. After reprimands from his parents, first Father, then Mother, he decided to give the video his attention. However, through the act of observing himself in the video he became excited, and through his excitement came a 'sustained attention', demonstrated in the way he started to verbally and non-verbally express his reflections, as the following scene shows:

80 *Video modalities as a psychological technique*

Image/Clip time Clip 6–7: 04:46–10:30	Verbal transcript
 (a)  (b)  (c)	R.: So tell me Alex, what's going on? Ch. Alex (via translator) …Oooh! I hit the ball so it's going er er diagonally and so Daddy almost couldn't catch the ball. …R.: What's happening there? Child Alex: Green! (responds in English) R.: Green. So do you use different coloured balls (there are other coloured balls visible in the extract we are watching) … Ch. (nods) And how do you decide which ones to use? Ch. Alex (via translator) Oh…daddy and I decide together

Figure 4.4(a–c) Hong Kong, researcher footage – Video for reflection and sustaining children's attention.

Non-verbal conduct – observation transcript extract

Alex watches the footage, talks and using his hands to express.
Alex speaks very loudly and quickly as he watches this footage informing us about what was going on, as we all watch.
He whispers in CC's ear and then in the researcher's ear, so that dad does not hear him say that he was trying to catch daddy out in the game.

Not only did Alex express himself linguistically, but through gesture. For example, as he observed himself in the video, he provided a physical demonstration of how he would often shut his eyes whilst holding up his arms to hit the ball because, as he says, 'I was a bit afraid…'

Image/Clip time Clip 7: 10:25–10:30	Verbal transcript
 *Figure 4.5* Hong Kong, Researcher footage: Video for reflection and transforming children's reflections through sustained attention.	Ch. Alex (via translator) Oh.... I close my eyes and I hit the ball and then I open my eyes again and look back R.: Oh is that what you did just now? Ch. Alex (via translator): Yes; I always do this R.: Why is that? Ch. Alex (via translator): Oh!. because the ball almost hit me.... I was a bit afraid..... ...

Non-verbal conduct – observation transcript

Demonstrates visually with hands clasped above his head as he shows how he hits the ball with his eyes closed
And then whispers what he did into the translator's ear.
Demonstrates how the ball was coming in his direction

As Alex gave the extract more attention, his interpretation and reflections of the interaction with his father transformed. For example, he told us about how they made decisions together, how he tried to catch his dad out (to mislead him in the game), and he talked about his reflections beyond the present by referring to the past, contrary to the notion that '...a child at this age cannot speak of anything but what is happening before his eyes or what he hears' (Vygotsky and Cole 1978: 263). Whilst giving attention to reflecting on the video was probably mediated by his warm relationship with the translator, evident in their smiles and whispered exchanges, the video being used for reflection had both an affective and cognitive response of sustained attention, transforming how he interpreted what he saw in the 'mirror'. This is a reflexive process. Through the image content being turned back to focus on Alex, he experienced and demonstrated an affective and cognitive response. Most importantly the kind of image drawing in his attention transformed his verbal interpretation of what was going on in his reflections. This has implications for researchers (and teachers who research) interested in child's positionality in relation to using video in its reflective modality and the content which is 'mirrored' to children.

But the affective and cognitive consequence of using video for reflection, particularly with young children, can also raise ethical questions about using this modality with young children. The following example illustrates this concern:

Case study example 4: England – Mr and Mrs Barker: activity setting, mealtimes

The example below is taken from researcher footage. It was a recording of a video extract being played back to Bea for her reflections. Bea was the youngest member (4 years old) of a family in England. The extract was of the family eating supper, during which father teased his youngest child, Bea, and she became cross. In this reflective use of video, Bea is watching the video extract with her older sister, Bell, and both parents:

R:	So Bea, why did you get cross? Can you tell me why you got cross? [Bea doesn't say anything but watches the video with us]
F:	I think Bea wanted to say something, or she wanted, and we were saying you can't.... she wanted to ask a question I think, and then we say, you can't ask a question until you have eaten some of your tea [supper]
R:	I know that Bell (who is elder sibling) said um, 'Daddy's joking with you'
Bell [Eldest sibling]:	You always say, 'Are you joking with me?', don't you Bea?
Bea:	[Silently shakes head in disagreement]
Bell:	Yes you do...Yes, she wanted to know if Dad had actually had Maltesers [for lunch], and Mummy would only tell her if she ate. Ah Bea... [Bea's expression changes, she is about to cry, as she stares at the reflection of herself being played back on the screen in front of her].
R:	What's the matter sweetheart?
F:	Ah Bea don't get upset darling, ah gosh...
Bell:	Ah, no....
F:	Give me a cuddle.
R:	[whispers to F] Why is she upset?
F:	I guess she's not used to seeing things played back
M:	Yes, tell R. about the Bea book
F:	Oh yes.
Bell:	That has things... that might just make Bea more upset, because that has things, like silly things that Bea has said... because sometimes, uh, she thinks that we're laughing at her, so she got upset...

(Family 1 England: Corbett Family;
Researcher footage – Film elicitation interview 1)

In the above scene, Bea began the interview eagerly watching the video extract with us, ready to reflect on what she was watching. There was no uncertainty in the situation. However, as she began to watch it, I could see her facial expression indicating a sense of uncertainty. She watched the video excitedly expecting to talk about it, and at the same time, watching it affected how she felt, so she decided not to speak. Responding through reflection therefore becomes changed by the very act of watching the film, and this can transform how young children interpret the footage for the researcher with both positive and negative outcomes.

Discussion

I began the chapter explaining how a research problem led to a methodological study about using video modalities in educational research. As researchers our team were interested in children's opportunities for development as part of understanding their potential through family interactions, and we focussed on father–child interactions. However, the children were young, and this posed a methodological problem. The study used video in an extractive modality to analyse learning as it develops through father–child interaction and identify opportunities for development from a cultural-historical perspective of human development. In this respect our use of video in its extractive modality expands researcher understanding about the relationship between theory and method in educational research, particularly in studies of human development. However, there are also further theoretical and methodological connections to this study, linked to the methodological theory of Double Stimulation.

Connections with methodological interpretations of the theory of double stimulation

Double stimulation – its origins, a method of experimental investigation

The origins of double stimulation lie in Vygotsky's 'waiting experiment'. In the classic waiting experiment (Sannino and Laitinen 2015), a clock serves as a second stimulus. Two types of stimuli, that is, the task (to wait in a room) and the clock, serve the purpose of objectifying inner psychological processes to trace the development of higher mental functions and reveal their structure (effectively it explicates both that the subject has agency but also how s/he decides what to do). However, the principle of double stimulation remains underdeveloped in application.

Sannino (2015a) paved the way for further thought using the concept, stating;

> Contemporary literature, ...seldom goes beyond brief accounts, primarily centred around the experimental design with two stimuli and limited domains of investigation. Also many contemporary studies

attribute different connotations and scopes to double stimulation. A thorough examination of the contemporary and classic literature leads me to consider underestimated aspects, which may enrich our understanding of double stimulation and open up interesting new avenues for further research.

(1)

For Sannino (2015a), double stimulation is not just a method, but also a principle of volition, which distinctively characterises all higher mental functions. She maintained that although the second stimuli plays a mediating function, what seems to be neglected in discussion is the importance of the conflict of motive, because that is what explicates volition. She therefore characterised double stimulation as containing conflictual aspects (represented as two stimuli). From Sannino's (2015a) position then, double stimulation can be seen as the conflict of motives that propel intentionality, which in turn affects the subject's behaviour.

> Conflict of motives denotes a clash between opposite aspirations or tendencies which occur in situations involving uncertainty about the situation …requiring the courage of deliberate choice.
> (Sannino 2015a: 8)

Sannino's more contemporary version of the waiting experiment is therefore based on the idea that there is a conflict between the motives of staying in the room – because of 'obedience, following rules, behaving in accepted ways, and feeling commitment due to contractual obligation' (Thorne 2015: 63) – and leaving the room, when the expected script does not happen. Most importantly:

> The power of the …experiment is that this conflict of motives evokes complex behaviours and forms of decision making, which in turn shed light on the human condition in the areas of intentionality and agency.
> (Thorne 2015: 15)

In a contemporary version, creating innovative second stimuli, such as measuring time or linking the time to their life activities (in Sannino's repeated experiment), participants created support for new courses of action, such as deciding 'I'm going to leave at a particular time'. This indicates how participants can transform a situation (Béhague et al 2008), influencing both themselves and their circumstances. So what does this have to do with the use of video?

The value of double stimulation to using video

In capturing the elements of a child's social situation through video's extractive modality, our research team were able to historically trace the dialectic conditions linked to conflict of motives, previously hidden from visibility, through which the child's higher mental functions (for example, strategic decision making) emerged. In this respect, combining double stimulation as a theory, with video in the extractive modality helped us (as researchers) to ask the kinds of questions which can make the non-visible visible. In doing so, they indicated the child's opportunities for development or, put another way, microgenetic 'moments' or 'turning points' that generate the kind of 'qualitative transformation' (Vygotsky and Cole 1978: 73), enabling development to be seen in a new way.

Using video in a reflection modality was also useful and seemed to function as an auxiliary stimulus (in this case propelling children's volitional actions) when young children had difficulties with giving and sustaining attention (Leont'ev 1932/1994; Vygotsky 1929/1979). We found that as young children observed their video extracts, there was often a dialectic between what they felt (an affective experience), what they saw as the footage, and how they responded emotionally in terms of visible behaviour (part of the affective). These former two elements sat together as a conflict of motives to help the children form decisions about responding and in turn their external behaviours. Whilst watching the footage (a task as a first stimulus so to speak), their affective response and associated intention changed and, in turn, so did their interpretation, because of the affective and cognitive consequences directly brought about through observing themselves in the video. Video used in a reflective modality with young children therefore demonstrated how the very act of young children observing themselves in video directly produces affective and cognitive consequences, transforming how they articulate and position their reflections. In this respect the video also functioned as a second auxiliary stimulus helping them to make decisions about how to interpret what they were watching.

Combining double stimulation with video for reflection addresses the main criticism of video use with children, that is, that there is a danger of viewing the visual as a neutral vehicle for arriving at the child's voice. By back tracing outward behaviour, it is possible to reflexively reveal how the very act of reflection as a video modality can involve a conflict of motives, which has both affective and cognitive consequences with implications for the kinds of research data yielded. It also raises ethical questions about using video in its reflective modality with vulnerable human beings, given the affective consequences might be a state of distress. Since video used in its reflective modality has both affective and cognitive consequences, I would urge researchers to be cautious when using this modality with vulnerable human beings.

Implications for video modalities and researching learner agency

Within our research community, video not only has an ambiguous status, but there remains a lack of understanding about its potential (Haw and

Hadfield 2011). The case illustrations in this chapter extends researcher understanding about using video in two modalities. Using video for extraction enabled the research team to contribute to the build-up of studies showing video's relationship with theory and method in research designs (in this study video for extraction was linked with a theory of human development). Using video for reflection in our study demonstrated how video is a way of explicating positioning from which participants 'speak', in this case young children. In this respect using video for reflection has the potential to be a reflexive tool in research design, to validate and support claims researchers make.

One of the unintended consequences of using video for extraction to study child development was how the analysis of conditions within extracts, demonstrating the child's perspective, also revealed agentive characteristics in children. Positioned from a dialectical perspective, the concept of agency was not independent from examining conditions for which development could occur. Rather, apparent oppositional positions (the situational in relation to the individual, and the conflict of motives they produce) form a dialectic framework, which work together through the act of agency. The agentive potential of the learner is therefore made visible through video analysis of dialectic interpersonal relationships as part of the child's social situation. We found as we used video for extraction to capture the child's social situation to identify opportunities for development, we also made agency visible. This is in line with some of the developing definitional work about agency from cultural historical researchers (Rainio and Hilppö 2017; Waermö 2016); namely that agency requires addressing both sociological and psychological dimensions:

> ...when researching agency ethnographically, the situatively emergent (sociological) and the temporarily developing (psychological) views, which in literature often stay separate, should be combined....our approach suggests that these apparently oppositional theoretical stances actually constitute each other within the concept of agency and therefore form a dialectical unity. ...Ethnographic data should be analysed on these two levels simultaneously: (a) on the level of micro-interaction where the social reality is situationally constructed and (b) on the developmental level to grasp the continuity and development of these situational manifestations of agency.
>
> (Rainio and Hilppö 2017: 83)

From this perspective there is a notion of a dialectical concept of agency (Rainio 2010) as part of the study of relational dialectics (Baxter and Montgomery 1996) and in our research, examining child development through researching children's social situation demonstrated a dialectical concept of agency. By implication the ways in which agency becomes possible in pedagogical relationships from a dialectical framework is widened, allowing children to be supported in learning, and for researchers it has implications for how they study learner agency. The methodology for this study also used video for reflection to gather children's interpretations when they were tasked with commenting on video extracts. Commenting on video extracts (stimulated recall) in research is nothing new. However, one of the unintended methodological findings from this study was how using video in its reflective modality with young children provides insights into affective and cognitive consequences young children display with this modality, as a consequence of 'the mirror effect' on themselves. This might be because using video for reflection is both reflexive and dialectic (Pink 2021), but clearly the content of images presented in the 'mirror' has implications for using video for reflection in studies with young children, which include ethical considerations.

Conclusion

Researching interactions, agency and their relation to human or child development, does require contextually and dynamically sensitive methods. Such methods make it possible to capture processes of development alongside the insider's perspective, given that from a cultural-historical or socio-cultural perspective, they are part of the conditions making up the person's social situation; and all of this is underpinned by a context; in this study, it was families. This is an ambitious and complex research endeavour. However, video in certain modalities, has potential to address those complexities and open possibilities. In the chapter, I shed light on those possibilities through my reflections of methodological issues raised when using video for extraction and video for reflection, as a psychological technique to study child development qualitatively. Whilst the chapter specifically relates to a study about child development, the way in which video in its extractive modality can 'capture' development processes and agency indicates it could be used in studies interested in the psychological study of human development and agency more generally. That might include, for example, researching developmental processes occurring through interactions between teachers, parents, pupils, peers or children, from a cultural-historical perspective of human development.

Notes

1 An international team of academics from the UK, India, Norway and Hong Kong.
2 This is a concept that encapsulates the notion of 'activity' (Leont'ev 1932/1994) as a collective mediating device. Here the unit of analysis is the activity setting, which involves the target child and the social and material conditions of which s/he is a part during interactions.

3 We make a distinction between footage and data (c.f. Erickson 2011). Our data is the conceptually led extracts from footage of everyday father–child interaction in family activity settings.
4 To introduce the filming task, I conducted a children's filmmaking training session with children in each family and provided them with a set of filmmaking equipment.
5 Parents granted permission to show faces for this paper because the data is not sensitive.

5 Transformative visual representations in interventionist methodology
Seeing is thinking in the change laboratory

Introduction

The chapter discusses the part visual representations play in the 'Change Laboratory' (CL) (Engeström 1987/2015), an interventionist approach to research in the Cultural, Historical Activity Theory (CHAT) tradition. CL offers a historically grounded account of how transformative collective practices produce and are produced through social interaction and human selves. In the chapter I demonstrate how knowledge about practice is built up and transformed collaboratively through thinking in pictures in CL. Specifically, I argue that CL as an intervention approach to social science problems uses visual representations transformatively by combining the study of social context, process and change, and in doing so practitioners come to understand and transform their work activity, collectively.

As a method, CL, applied to interventionist studies of transformation in work (Engeström, Lompscher and Rückriem 2005; Engeström 2007), poses questions associated with the development of self within social practice. It also aims to develop work practices and addresses problems in work-based learning and learning at work generally (Engeström 1987/2015; Engeström et al. 1996; Daniels 2001; Virkkunen and Newnham 2013). Its contexts lie in a range of school-related studies and research problems, such as promoting professional practice to tackle unequal access to educational success (Spante et al. 2022); vocational schooling (Teräs and Lasonen 2013) and the development of teacher or learner agency (Sannino 2010; Englund and Price 2018; Morselli and Sannino 2021). It is often used by a team of practitioners, with the help of an interventionist (Engeström 1987/2015, 2007). For the development of academic theory, CL has the advantage of being a theoretically informed approach for professional collaborative learning and development (Engeström, Lompscher and Rückriem 2005; Engeström 2007), and at a practical level, it is suited to facilitating change in educational practice, through collaboration.

DOI: 10.4324/9781003000549-5

In the chapter I discuss and reflect on using visual representations in CL by drawing on a study about Father Groups, which I conducted as part of evaluating a local poverty alleviation programme for children and families in England, known as Sure Start[1]. The Father Group study aimed to facilitate practitioners' work in transforming how fathers became involved in child development. I conducted the project with a team of practitioners in two stages. Stage One, the ethnographic stage, examined the way practitioners interpreted and supported father involvement through ethnographic case studies of their 'father groups'. Stage Two involved CL, whose methodology is delivered through a series of DWR (development work research) workshops. DWRs used visual representations to present aspects of CHAT. They represented the temporal aspect of CHAT, recording practitioners' context of practice; from past to present reflections of processes; explicating tensions in practice which I as the interventionist used to facilitate change for future practice. In this methodological chapter, I focus on how visual representations worked in the CL stage of the study, demonstrating how they combined the study of context, process and change to transform practitioners' understanding of their work activity.

The chapter is divided into three parts. Part one provides an overview of CL as an intervention approach when considered alongside an alternative, action research. Action research is a commonly used research approach in education which uses interventions to promote change. How then is CL different? Part two provides an account of the Fathers Group project and its research design. Part three reflects on using visual representations in CL for the study, and the conclusion summarises my methodological reflections. I maintain CL is a rare example of a qualitatively driven mixed methods intervention approach to research, in which visual representations help participants and practitioners transform their understanding about the relationship between their work, its context, processes and change, whilst at the same time participating in the intervention approach themselves.

Interventions, educational research and Change Lab. (CL) methodology

Amongst educational researchers, action research is established as an intervention approach (see, for example, Kemmis and McTaggart 2005). CL intervention, on the other hand, is a lesser-known intervention methodology to those scholars who do not work within a cultural historical perspective. CL differs from action research in several ways. It is rooted in the cultural historical activity theory tradition (CHAT), the theory of 'Expansive Learning' (Engeström 1987/2015) and DWR methodology. Based on concepts and principles of re-mediation and double stimulation (see, for example, Sannino 2015a, 2015b; Sannino et al 2016; Chawla-Duggan et al. 2022),

Transformative visual representations 91

derived from CHAT (Leont'ev 1978; Engeström 1987/2015; Cole and Engeström 2007), there are differences between its approach to intervention when compared to action research. Differences include the unit of analysis, its ontological and epistemological basis and its relationship to theory, in particular its adaptation of Vygotsky's (1978) concept of the zone of proximal development (ZPD).

Unit of analysis: activity system(s) and activity theory

One of the most explicit differences between action research and CL is CL's direct connection with CHAT as a theoretical perspective. From this perspective, CL uses a theoretical unit of analysis known as the activity system (or several activity systems)[2]. This idea sits in contrast to the ways in which researchers sometimes explain a social system as having certain empirical characteristics. In contrast...

> In a ...Change Laboratory... the basic unit of analysis for development is an activity system or combination of interdependent activity systems. This concept comprises a theoretical generalization about the inner structure and dynamics of an activity that explains its change and the way an intervention can affect it.
>
> (Virkkunen and Newnham 2013: 32)

The model suggests the possibility of analyzing a multitude of relations within the triangular structure of activity. However, the essential task is always to grasp the systemic whole, not just separate connections.

(Engeström 2015: 62)

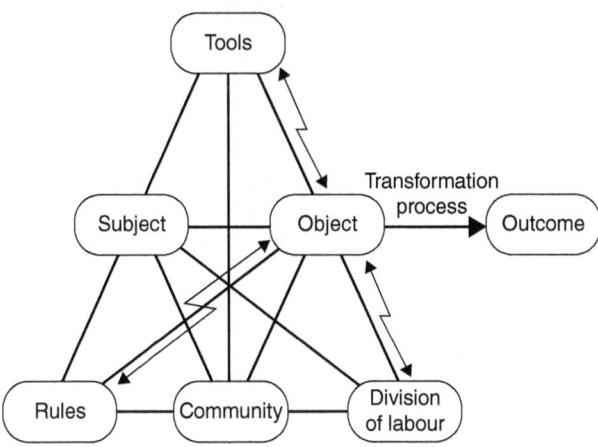

Figure 5.1 The activity system with contradictions indicated. (Adapted from Cole and Engeström 1993: 36).

Engeström's triangle is a diagram of a systemic representation of[3] Leont'ev's (1978) activity approach, sometimes known as second generation CHAT (2 GAT). Engeström (2015) presented this triangular heuristic to use in analysis in early work (see Engeström 1987), explaining how human activity is organised systemically and transformations occur historically.

A key assumption underpinning activity theory and a cultural historical activity system (as a theory of mind) is how human activity is a cultural system. From this perspective of Activity Theory, human-mediated activity represents the basic unit of analysis when studying human behaviour; and human contributions to life activity has, is and continues to evolve through transforming how human activity is organised systemically. This is a complex idea, but the main theoretical concept in CL is the model of how human activity is organised systemically. The model, 2GAT, is based on one in which Leont'ev identified how human action can be a collective activity rather than an individual action. In 2GAT the unit of analysis changes from Vygotsky's idea of tools (Vygotsky and Cole 1978) that mediate joint activity (Blunden 2010) to 'object-oriented activity' (Van der veer and Valsiner 1991).

A dialectic ontology

Whilst Engeström's (2007) diagram of the activity system depicts how human activity is organised systemically, showing its systemic relations, it is the contradictions within the system that propel change, and in this respect, there is a dialectic[4] mechanism at work, which drives change.

A key concept of activity theory is therefore 'contradictions' which is understood as a dialectic mechanism[5]; and this is essentially the idea underpinning Engeström's (1987/2015) notion of expansive learning in which:

> Within the structure of any specific productive activity, the contradiction is renewed as the clash between individual actions and the total activity system...The two directions or 'opposite starting points', from within an activity and from between two activities, are essential for the emerging concept of expansion....
>
> (Engeström 2015: 66–67)

The philosophical basis underpinning the notion of contradictions is its ontological position, that is, its understanding of how reality exists. Here reality consists of dialectical processes of self-propulsion as a mechanism for movement. In its practical application, CL methodology uses the mechanism of movement which strives to overcome contradictions between the individual and the total activity system. Therefore, its methodology lies in its connection with a dialectic view of human activity, and the development of human activities and consciousness of the self, occurring as part of change. In action research there is no assumption of a dialectic to explain how social reality exists, in a relation between our internal and external worlds, and how we intellectually evolve as human beings. In this study the overall dialectic led to the expansion of practitioners' understanding of context, process and change in their work. In this respect, the visual representations helped to make explicit their understanding of reality and its possibilities.

Object orientation – an epistemological basis

Unlike action research, the driving force underpinning the collective work of practitioners working in CL is, epistemologically speaking, linked to the relational concept of object-oriented activity. The object of activity is a central concept in this framework because different kinds of activity are distinguished by their objects. The object facilitates the kind of knowledge constructed, as it defines what it is you are trying to change. From the AT perspective, it is always linked to motive or need:

> An entity can only become an object of activity when it meets a need and is invested with the meaning and motivating power related to meeting that need. Needs in society evolve as inner contradictions within and between activity systems...
> (Virkkunen and Newnham 2013: 35)

In other words, the entity out there in the environment becomes the object of an activity when it meets a need and is invested with meaning and motivating power. In this respect, objects have a 'motivating force' (Leont'ev 1978: 54) and refer to something at which we as human beings direct:

> ...The main thing that distinguishes one activity from another... is the difference of their objects. It is exactly the object of an activity that gives it a determined direction...The object of an activity is its true motive. The motive may be either material or ideal, either present in perception or existing only in imagination or in thought.
> (Leont'ev 1978: 62)

Since the 'object' is connected to meeting a need, it is an entity that is always historically developing, which means we can potentially transform the object of an activity through our actions.

The concept of object-oriented activity is therefore not to be confused with the idea of 'objectives', often associated with teachers' curriculum planning, 'Object' from a dialectic position is a term which is part of a mediational relationship within the activity system, rather than something which stands on its own or is linked with objectives. It is concerned with knowing about what knowledge you are working on 'shifting', to achieve an outcome. From a researcher's perspective, CL, as an intervention, observes human engagement with problem solving and is therefore concerned with how we work out what we need to 'shift'[6] as part of knowledge construction. In contrast, the focus in action research is usually about the performance of problem solving (what we need to do to address the problem). As a result, action research contributes to the gradual development of a practice connected to a visible problem or seeks to realise a predefined objective (Virkkunen and Newnham 2013). CHAT, on the other hand, forms the basis for development towards a future collective object, which is constructed according to a historical and contemporary analyses of a practice. A collective object (we might call this a common object) for a group of practitioners gives direction for the actions conducted by individual people or a team. This means that focused sub-questions in research, derived from an overall research question for the whole group, can frame the activity in its setting. So, for example, development in groups of practitioners can be in line with institutional development demands and goals (such as in a school or organisation). Research within CHAT therefore treats people as systems within a system of social relations and, in this respect, the dialectic ontology underpinning CL consists of relational concepts, which at a practical level, are positioned in contradiction for movement to occur.

The role of theory

Connections with institutional culture and Vygotsky's (1978) concept of ZPD

The CL process (Engeström 1996b) implements what Engeström (1987/2015) refers to as a 'cycle of expansive learning'. Through the cycle, practitioners engage in reflective cycles of deconstruction, reconstruction, trial and re-adjustment. It is a participatory approach to interventionist research in which the objective is to reveal the needs and possibilities for development in an activity, not in relation to a given objective, but by jointly constructing the 'zone of proximal development' (Vygotsky and Cole 1978) of the activity:

> Expansive development research aims at making cycles of expansive transition collectively mastered journeys through zones of proximal development.
>
> (Engeström 1987/2015: 263)

Transformative visual representations 95

In his theory of expansive learning, Engeström (1987/2015) essentially adapted Vygotsky's individual-oriented concept of the ZPD to collective activities, writing,

> It is the distance between the present everyday actions of the individuals and the historically new form of the societal activity that can be collectively generated as a solution to the double bind potentially embedded in the everyday actions.
>
> (Engeström 1987/2015: 138)

In an institutional sense this means that both the activity and the culture of the institution (for example, a school) are developed and changed. The intention is then that all practitioners collectively develop a shared 'object' and act on it. This is different from action research, where the aim is more often about developing the practices of one or a few practitioners (Cochran-Smith and Lytle 2009; Kemmis and Mctaggart 2005; McNiff 2016).

Practical cycle of expansive developmental research

An expansive developmental research methodology (Engeström 2015: 253) also underpins CL's practical application. A methodological cycle for expansion occurs through several steps. Whilst there are critiques as to whether the process is actually cyclical (Augustsson 2021), the steps (Engeström 2015) are generally as follows:

1 *Phenomenology; delineation*:
   The first step is essentially a process of shedding light onto an area of study, problems experienced by practitioners, and the researcher's initial understanding of contradictory conditions giving rise to practitioners' concerns. It may often be accomplished through an ethnographic analysis of the current situation (through participant on-site observations and discussions with those involved in the activity (Engeström 2015: 254)).
2 *Analysis of activity*:
   In the second step, there is an analysis of the activity system through three processes.
   First an object historical analysis, in which the activity model helps to uncover contradictions in the system that have led to transitions of the 'object' historically. Here the focus is essentially on 'finding the object'.
   Second, a historical analysis occurs. This aspect of analysis assumes there are always tools (e.g., handbooks, timetables, instructions) which

function as conceptual instruments in practical activity. Development phases (or internal change processes) use those conceptual instruments as part of the process. The main aim of this aspect of analysis is 'to identify and trace how a second set of contradictions come about and connect to the secondary instruments for successive developmental issues' (Engeström 2015: 256).

The final process is empirical analysis, which aims to reveal inner contradictions, where the participants as part of the activity face the second set of contradictions:

> This can be achieved by letting the participants reconstruct the analysis through their own actions. Such a reconstruction typically takes place on the basis of selected ... materials as well as tasks involving debate between the participants.
>
> (Engeström 2015: 256)

3 *Formation of new instruments*:
Engeström (2015) refers to the third step as 'dramatic in expansive methodology', in that participants are pushed into forming a new model of their activity to re-solve contradictions for transition to occur.

4 *Practical application of new instruments to change the activity*.
In the penultimate step, new instruments are implemented in selected strategic tasks. The tasks represent breakthroughs which advance practice and 'the participants of the activity system face intense conflicts and contradictions between the old and the given new ways of doing and thinking...' (Engeström 2015: 261). Conflicts can be in several forms, for example, between old rules (again refer to Figure 5.1) and a new instrument or tool, or old division of labour and new communication. The task of the intervention-based research is to trace and analyse solutions to conflicts produced by the participants.

5 *Reporting*:
In the final step Engeström (ibid.: 262) advises researchers to use a historico-genetic method for presenting findings. This is essentially about reproducing the actual course of the expansive transition as a journey of learning to solve a problem, with its temporal structure. 'This type of reporting has ancestors...in the genres of the diary, ...the travel story and the developmental novel' (ibid.: 263).

The Study, CHAT and the Change Lab. (CL)

Background and rationale for CHAT and CL

The study took place at a time when wider UK policy agenda for supporting children through families highlighted a gap in provision supporting fathering. Policy documentation stipulated the need for more support to help parents play a critical role in supporting children's development, and they specifically mentioned activities for fathers. Such policy drew attention to the idea that state/public service provision for children and families in England did not adequately connect with the context of fathers' lives or motivations; and practitioners underestimated the significance of a father's involvement if he was not visible to the service, or not living with the child. Such policy proposed a 'culture change' in public services by changing the way services worked to ensure they reached and supported father involvement. This was the policy context at the time of the study. At that time I was evaluating Sure Start provision in a Southwest region of England and I noticed a lack of published academic knowledge and understanding about how practitioners were actually engaging with fathers through Father groups. This was the impetus for researching father groups.

Accordingly, the study aimed to understand and facilitate practitioners' work in supporting father involvement through their groups by practically implementing Engeström's (1987/2015) CL within the CHAT theoretical tradition.

I adopted CHAT for several reasons. First, I believed a CHAT perspective allowed me to understand, explain and facilitate shifts in human thinking, and was touching a deeper level of understanding for sustained changes in practice. Second, using a CHAT approach provided an analytic device, one which allowed me as a social science researcher to theoretically explore how practitioners work together to produce outcomes. This becomes possible because CHAT points to the need to analyse tools/mediating artefacts used to do the work of change, and the object being worked on with these tools, along with the reasons, to achieve outcomes. Third, from a CHAT point of view, development takes place through resolving contradictions and tensions (which often have a historical short- or long-term root), and for me this had the added advantage of being able to understand situations through a longitudinal perspective, past, present and future. Therefore, I proposed a CHAT approach to address the following objectives:

a   To understand practitioners' current practice
b   To explain historical reasons informing current practice, and
c   To use dilemmas faced in current practice to inform future practice

For readers using a CL approach for the first time, the objectives above are a sound theoretically informed set of practical statements which can be adapted to your own research questions if they are related to researching collaborative development and/or work-based problems.

The project on Father groups occurred in two phases. Phase one explored ways in which practitioners interpreted and supported father involvement through ethnographic case studies of their groups. In phase two, I conducted CL through DWR workshops, as part of a 'Cycle of Expansive Learning' (Engeström 2007). Through the two phases CHAT suitably addressed the study's research objectives.

Object-oriented sampling strategy – Sampling for a common object

The study worked with a cluster sample of practitioners from three father groups with a common object. I did not initially expect to sample for a common object and for it to be part of a theoretical sampling strategy. My sampling strategy involved identifying and contacting all Sure Start sites delivering father groups in the South-west of England, informing them about the project's aims, with a view to finding out more about their groups. The process resulted in initial meetings with practitioners from eight groups in the southwest of England.

Several issues arose from analysing the semi-structured interviews represented in those initial meetings, issues which I only later realised provided an 'object oriented' (and therefore theoretically informed) sample of father group practitioners. This occurred because several practitioners I interviewed belonged to a regional practitioner forum, and they met regularly as members of the forum. From an activity theory perspective, I thought, given the practitioners already met regularly through the forum, the object of the study (what we were working on shifting) could become synonymous with the concerns of the forum group. Five of the forum members ran father groups, and in this study, I decided to investigate four of the groups in the first instance, with the fifth group practitioner joining us at the workshop stage, to identify the extent to which the issues and solutions raised applied across all the groups. This strategy was a way of addressing limited availability the fifth group practitioner had at the time of the study.

A second advantage of working with a cluster sample was it allowed me to look at father involvement and its promotional support in a particular cultural context (in this study it was white, working class fathers). I envisaged future work might sample for common objects across a diverse population of socio-economic status.

Data collection and analysis

Whilst the first phase of the study collected data through ethnographic case studies of four father groups, using participant observation and semi-structured interviews, the second, more specific phase involved preparing for the CL intervention. It included collecting data needed for planning the intervention and creating a mirror of the work activity for practitioners in the CL. It also included scheduling a sequence of CL sessions.

Phase 1: The ethnographic phase

The ethnographic phase included:

- Weekly participant observation of practitioner–father interaction in four groups (normally each of the groups met for one morning a week) over a period of 4 months.
- Monthly semi-structured 1:1 interviews with four practitioners, and group interviews with fathers from each of the four father groups.

Phase one focused on exploring practitioners' existing ideas and practice about father involvement by attending weekly sessions over a period of 4 months, where I took on the role of participant observer. Whilst I initially selected a role of observer as participant where the researcher does not enter a sustained relationship with informants in order to simply view what was 'going on', I gradually took on the role of participant as observer (I was in fact the breakfast sandwich maker). This observation continuum allowed me to observe and ask questions over time, as part of the setting. I recorded father group observations in a field diary and included dates, times and contents of sessions observed. I used the data to subsequently frame questions for semi-structured interviews in relation to the AT framework. For example, after observing sessions, I asked practitioners about what they were working on in those sessions, where they wanted to be, and the kinds of tensions they experienced between the two, or issues which helped or hindered what they were working on.

I analysed data collected from the 'ethnographic' orientated phase in terms of the AT framework. In doing so, the analysis identified several tensions in terms of where practitioners wanted to go when related to their existing conditions. Methodologically, that meant, in terms of an activity framework, I was trying to identify whether there was actually a *common object* they were all working on, for father involvement.

Table 5.1 identifies the directions of the different groups in terms of what practitioners wanted to work on in relation to their existing conditions and the tensions it raised for them.

As Table 5.1 demonstrates, concerns overlapped into potential common objects. One common object was related to the issue of practitioners recognising there are differences in how fathering is played out, to address a similar problem, and to try to subsequently raise this understanding with the men in their group.

Phase 2: Conducting DWR Workshops – CL

To prepare for the CL intervention I introduced practitioners to the second phase of the study early in the first phase, recognising how one phase

Table 5.1 Practitioners' directions and tensions

Whose group?	Direction(s) and tensions
Will	Tensions: concern over ideal perceptions of fathering vs. actual fathering and how to support the actual; also concern between fathers' values vs. practitioners' values
Pete	Trying to get fathers to run the group themselves/to take responsibility vs. practitioners making the decisions
Ted	Concern over child development/socialisation practices; practitioners want fathers to reflect on their own experience of being fathers vs. how were they (the dads) fathered
Ernest and Jackie	Tension: concern over universal vs. actual/particular fathering; underpinned by the practitioner belief that we cannot treat all fathers the same, for the same concerns (one size does not fit all).

informs the other. From a researcher's perspective, the idea in this kind of intervention research is to observe how humans engage with problem solving. To undertake the process, it is important for participants to be familiar with their engagement 'tool'. Therefore, I gave initial briefings about the CL method to familiarise practitioners with the language of the activity system, as a tool for transformation. Accordingly, I presented a short paper to practitioners at the ethnographic phase of data collection, so they could be clear on the kinds of questions I would ask when examining the observation data and in talking with them (whilst also acknowledging other issues may arise outside of questions directly related to the AT system, but which might be indirectly related). At the beginning of the first DWR, that is, Workshop 1, I once again discussed the AT systemic tool. In this way, I kept practitioners familiar with the AT system as a theoretical and heuristic device with which they could work.

The second phase aimed to:

i) Investigate the extent to which there were contradictions between existing practice on the one hand, and on the other hand, what practitioners actually wanted, and the reasons for mismatches.

ii) Identify implications for future practice to support father involvement. Phase 2 involved:
- Using data to create a mirror of current practice, scheduling and conducting four DWR workshops with practitioners, drawing on ethnographic evidence, explanations for current practices and questions about existing practice for the development of alternative ideas for future practice.

- Videotaping DWR workshops as we conducted them, for the purpose of reflection, analysis of practice and development of future practice, in follow-up workshops.

I conducted four DWR workshops over a period of six months and planned each session based on the AT analysis of preceding sessions.

Visual representations and the three screens

A central tool in setting up CL is a set of three screens for representing work activity, which participants face alongside each other (Engeström 2007: 370–371). The three screens represent work activity where movement occurs in three dimensions (underpinned by a notion of time: what has happened in the past, the present and future plans). The three screens, respectively, present data, ideas and a systemic diagram based on activity theory. During DWR workshops practitioners work with the researcher (as interventionist) and three screens, known as the mirror screen, the AT diagram and the ideas screen. In this study I used two flip charts as screens (for the ideas and systemic diagram) and a digital projector screen (for a mirror data screen).

During DWR workshops I presented combinations of video data, participant observations and semi-structured interview data as 'mirror data' (Engeström 2007) on the mirror screen. Mirror data represented practitioners' work practices and contradictions upon which they continually reflected. I positioned the mirror data screen in between the AT systemic diagram and ideas screens. This enabled the AT theory and analysis to inform one another. It also enabled practitioners to visibly see the research intervention process at work, moving between areas of practice through theory and development through theory, as I incorporated subsequent mirror data into follow-up workshop sessions. I delivered workshops in situ (the practitioner's place of work), a requirement of this form of intervention (Engeström 2007), and video recorded the workshops, using the material as further mirror data to reflect upon in future workshops.

Logistically, when arranging the CL, I positioned the camera and its movement carefully to ensure all practitioners were included in frames. This allowed for both verbal and non-verbal responses to be included in video footage. Videotaping the sessions allowed me to analyse how the expansive learning journey progressed in the session by analysing the video recording. I identified emerging themes, discussed them with the practitioners involved, noting appearances of inner contradictions in the activity system emerging through practitioners' discussions in the DWRs. Based on the analysis, I identified which themes required further explanation and evidence through mirror data and whether I would need to introduce certain analytic concepts (as mediating artefacts/tools) to facilitate practitioners in their expansive learning process.

102 *Transformative visual representations*

In the following section I explain how I worked with the three screens and practitioners in the DWR workshops to demonstrate how the three visual representations combined to facilitate practitioners' understanding of their work, in terms of its context, process and potential change.

The AT diagram: social context and knowledge construction

In DWR Workshop 1, I introduced the screen illustrating Engeström's AT diagram. I explained its purpose, giving examples of practical application in research projects:

> It tries to understand people's actions and learning in context in a way that the context is analysed at the same time as the actions. You can't look at the work of involving fathers without looking at the whole context of that work – what do you use? what do you work on? who is involved? whether you share the work or not; what the supports or constraints are, of the work? It helps if you think of work as an activity, which is why it's called activity theory.
>
> (DWR 1: Researcher (and facilitator) Video transcript)

The practitioners faced the activity diagram screen as I provided examples of studies in which the AT model was used. As part of familiarising practitioners with the AT diagram, I related it to how discussion would progress in workshops, linking it to the concept of 'object' in the diagram and how we would be 'following the object' through discussion. From a CHAT perspective, 'following the object' (as a problem space) is central because it determines the kind of knowledge being constructed, as it defines and redefines what it is practitioners are trying to work on, to achieve an outcome. I explained:

> Now the way I organise my questions and my analysis, is along these sort of lines, this triangle. I will keep reminding you of this triangle and use the language in this triangle in each workshop.
> (ALL PARTICIPANTS ARE WATCHING THE SCREEN OF THE AT DIAGRAM)
> I'm interested in what people are working on. What practitioners are working on. (Pauses)
> ...
> I'm going to be asking you that question and that's distinct from what you're trying to achieve. It's not to do with outcomes; it's to do with the 'object'.
> (Ernest makes notes)

One of the first things we want to get to grips with is the distinction between what you're working on (points to 'object' in AT diagram), and what you're trying to achieve and making that separation (points to 'outcomes' in the diagram). When we talk about what you're working on, I mean, is that what you're trying to change or shift?

(DWR 1: Researcher (as facilitator) Video transcript)

I continued to explain each aspect of the diagram, giving examples of its application, so participants became familiar about how the terms are defined and used. For example, when introducing the Vygotskian concept of tool as represented in the diagram, I proposed the following:

I have a diary. Most of us keep diaries. It's a clear example of a tool. When we're doing our work, most of us use diaries; they're not necessarily complicated, but without one I suspect most of us would fall apart. We use watches, we use earphones, we use all sorts of things...

A colleague of mine is doing a project with teachers who are trying to co-ordinate across schools...They were trying to make cross-school collaboration work for them and they couldn't get in touch with each other. It was things like "I rang but she's never there. I sent an email but she didn't get it"... Until they drew up a new timetable, a tool. So, 'X' would be near her place at 4.30 every Tuesday, at her desk if you wanted to get hold of her and that made a difference.

(DWR 1: Researcher (as facilitator) Video transcript)

At a more general level I explained how the aim of the series of workshops was to work with practitioners as they built their own theory of how practitioners do the work of father involvement through father groups (a theory of their work, so to speak). This would involve taking their everyday experience and building an AT model of that context and process. When referring to the AT diagram as a model, I raised the question of context once again, as part of considering the strategic direction of father groups, which at the time of the study were under threat as government funding for Sure Start programmes was slowly being redirected. A different system of devolved management and funding therefore threatened the continuation of their groups:

Now at a strategic level you might be able to say "OK this is what seems to work for practitioners doing the work of father involvement."
(JILL MAKES NOTES. EVERYONE IS WATCHING THE SCREEN OF THE AT DIAGRAM).
But we might ask ourselves if this model is specific to one of your groups? Because all the groups are different or is there stuff that's going on in these models that people are building on, in general. In

other words, are there things which would be general to Children's Centres/Sure Start Centres doing work on father involvement? Are there things that are common to you all as you build up your practice and the theory of the work you do in Father groups? This is the practice (RC-D points to mirror screen), and this is the theory (RC-D points to AT diagram screen).

(DWR 1: Researcher (as facilitator) Video transcript)

Having given considerable time to familiarising the group with a visual representation of the AT diagram and its concepts as a context for work activity, the task for DWR Workshop 1 was to generate the 'object' of practitioners' work. I provided practitioners with paper and explained the task:

> What I'd like you to do is write down what you're trying to change in your work in order to achieve...the sort of outcomes you want. Now we've said that the outcomes are to do with – involving fathers in their children's learning.... What are you trying to work on shifting in your work, to achieve that outcome ...?
>
> (DWR1 Task (from facilitator) Object identification)

The Ideas screen and the AT diagram – the role of the researcher as interventionist

We moved back and forth between screens to familiarise practitioners' understanding of the AT system, its concepts and their work activity. I used the ideas screen to list the 'objects' practitioners provided and to differentiate the concept of 'object' from 'outcome', whilst simultaneously referring to the AT diagram. As we discussed each of their statements defining their object, my role was to facilitate how they differentiated between 'object' and 'outcome'. In most cases their list appeared to be outcomes in the first instance, rather than objects, so as the interventionist, I facilitated identifying objects with them, as the following extract illustrates:

> RC-D (READS FROM PARTICIPANTS' LISTS OF OBJECTS; WRITES AN OBJECT FROM THE LIST ON IDEAS SCREEN)
> *Making groups more open to the possibility of more fathers coming in, by having male workers*
> So, is your outcome one in which you've got more fathers attending groups? So are you working on how the fathers perceive the group?
> (Pete strokes his chin and frowns. He folds his arms across his chest).
> Pete – A father friendly service.

RC-D – So are you working on changing how fathers see groups?
(Ernest nods)
Pete – Yeah, by having male workers, I would have said.
(Pete looks around the group for agreement).
(RC-D (WRITES ON IDEAS SCREEN) – *Outcome: more fathers in group.*
(Ernest and Pete watch)
(RC-D (READS NEXT 'OBJECT' FROM LIST)
That dads can contribute positively towards their children's learning....
So, what are we saying...we're changing family's understanding of what they do for children's learning?
(ERNEST LEANS FORWARD AND PUTS HIS HEAD IN HIS HANDS. HE SPEAKS WHILST GESTURING THROUGH HIS HANDS).
Ernest – No, it's about perception - changing father's perception of their role in children's learning.
(ERNEST LEANS FORWARD, ELBOWS ON TABLE, LINKS HIS FINGERS).
RC-D – So is it about changing how they see themselves as fathers, then? Are you working on notions of father identity?
Ernest – Yes.
(RC-D) (WRITES ON IDEAS SCREEN) Object - *Working on father identity...*
(RC-D (READS AND WRITES OUT NEXT OBJECT FROM LIST...)
(Video recording: DWR1 Task – Object identification)

Mirror screen, mirror data and the AT diagram: stimulating a historical, contextual understanding of processes

In a CL intervention, a researcher gathers 'mirror data' (Cole and Engeström 2007) to help practitioners develop an understanding of their processes of practice and, in doing so, expand their perspectives. By combining mirror screen reflections through the lens of the AT diagram, practitioners can start to see their work in ways they may have not seen their work activity before.

I introduced the mirror screen as DWR 1 progressed. The mirror screen contained ethnographic data from semi-structured interviews and participant observations of father groups. In subsequent DWR workshops, it also contained video material recorded from preceding DWR workshops.

Mirror screen data facilitated practitioners' reflections of current practice, and also to understand it in relation to historically rooted processes of their work in the activity system. For example, in the following illustration I chose an extract from the ethnographic data about men's attendance at fathers groups historically (keeping in mind that in the academic and practitioner literature, 'men' are traditionally positioned as 'hard to reach' in parental involvement programmes):

> EVERYONE LOOKS AT THE MIRROR SCREEN AND RC-D READS FROM IT.
> *I think it's the confidence within fathers to attend the activities of the group even though it is specifically aimed at dads; there is still that lack of confidence of what is expected of them when they get there. It's ongoing work, trying to get dads involved with the dads' group*
> (DWR 1 ethnographic interview data presented on mirror screen)

I went on to explain how I had interpreted the extract in terms of object and outcome, and they expanded on 'tools' used historically to recruit fathers to groups:

> RC-D: Now in this extract, involvement seems to be about getting them to attend in the first place. How do you get dads to attend (in this extract) because they don't know... what is expected of them when they get there? What it tends to suggest is that you're working on how they perceive the group. You can't get them to attend because they don't know what to expect...not confident about what it will be like. So do you have to work on how THEY see the group? Is that so?
> Pete – You have to sell them the group in a way. Because no-one really has an idea of what a fathers group can do.
> Ernest – It's as Pete says, if you put 'fathers group' on the tin it still doesn't tell you much, does it?
> RC-D READS ANOTHER INTERVIEW EXTRACT FROM THE MIRROR DATA SCREEN:
> *Everybody's experience will tell you that if you're not proactive in going out, meeting dads, setting up groups for them, working with them individually, generally...they're not able to bring people in. There's not enough staff, skills, time, the inclination to do work with dads.*
> RCD So what are the tools to make father involvement work happen?
> (Pete nods).
> (DWR 1: Mirror Screen data & the AT Diagram)

The reference to tools suggested we used mirror screen data in combination with their reflections to contextualise their work processes through the lens of the AT diagram.

Mirror and ideas screens: understanding processes

We also used the mirror and ideas screens in combination to extend a joint understanding of processes and to trigger further ideas about practitioner work processes on the ideas screen. In this next example, as practitioners reflect on mirror data, an idea emerges which is about what goes on for fathers when they are 'without' groups, but as a spin off from experiences 'within' groups, and vice versa:

> This last week, one dad has had a nightmare of a child protection issue. So he's been hauled over the coals and he's asked me to support him though it all - visits from Social Services and all the rest of it. It's been really, useful to him, I think, and that's been a spin-off for the group. (MIRROR SCREEN DATA).
> (RCD LOOKS AT ANNA WHO HAS HER HAND OVER HER MOUTH AND NODS).
>
> *Anna:* The real spin-offs come outside of the group. The fact that they come to the group is where the relationship is made and where the confidence is made, if you like. The dads can be quite supportive of one another.
> *Ernest:* I think the spin-offs, up until recently, have been individual, and now we're looking at it as a collective group... We've got these things going on in the group and outside of the group for this work on father involvement.
> (DWR 2: Mirror data and Idea Screen)

Practitioners reflected on the emerging idea of how change was working on both the external behaviour of fathers in their groups, alongside their internal problems, through the experiences of 'within and without the groups'. In discussing and explaining the process, they developed the idea of 'spin offs', as part of the father group experience generally. The CL process enabled practitioners to develop a collective understanding of the work of the different father groups and how they perceived and differentially handled 'spin offs' as a general issue. In this respect mirror and ideas screens worked together to generate, construct and extend a joint practitioner understanding of the processes of their work.

The role of the researcher-interventionist

- **Facilitating knowledge construction**

In my methodological notes I recorded my difficulties as a researcher in carrying DWR workshops. My difficulties pivoted on questions about conceptual development and my role as interventionist in facilitating practitioners' construction of knowledge. Such difficulties were played out in the workshop itself, but also later when analysing workshop video material in my attempts to create a mirror of their work activity for practitioners to reflect upon:

> Found it quite hard to think 'on the spot' in terms of relating their ideas to …concepts, analysis and methodology: it's quite a challenge …I read the data and automatically want to put a concept next to it, which is fine, but it needs to connect with the triangle….and with contradictory ideas emerging. So instead, I have to look at the data and ask myself 'what's this about' (in relation to the triangle…i.e. is it talking about the outcome (what's to happen), or the object (what you need to shift to get to the outcome) i.e. this isn't going to happen unless… and where are the contradictions?
>
> (RC-D diary notes)

I listed a series of questions to ask from the data as part of my AT analysis.

Analysis of AT data:
1 What's to happen (outcome)?
2 What's the object? This isn't going to happen unless (the shift) – object?
3 How do they share the work out (division of labour)?
4 Who's involved (community)?
5 What/how helps the work and hinders the work (rules, supports, constraints)?
6 Their tools (what are the tools to work on the shift)?

Such questions guided me through the analysis of DWR 1 and to prepare video extracts for Mirror data in DWR2.

- **Facilitating expansive learning actions**

    When analysing video recordings from DWR1, I identified main issues, and what needed to be developed through the activity system in DWR2. There were two aspects I planned for DWR 2, Part A and B.

In part A I wanted practitioners to prioritise an object from those they had identified in DWR1, with its historical association, that is, to identify the basis of the object from past experiences. I planned to probe whether historical roots were particular to their own father groups, or generally applicable, across the groups. In part B, I wanted to develop practitioners' understanding of tools within the AT system.

My extracted notes indicate my intervention plan for DWR2 on the basis of analysing DWR1:

- Facilitate practitioners to expand on what they have said by asking them to give past examples and its relation to success or failure on outcomes.
- Work on tools by looking at their relation to the object and gather past examples to get the practitioners to identify tools they use.
- What are the tensions between tools and objects?
- Pull out whether there are different activity theory models operating for the practitioners, or one. (RC-D diary DWR 2 intervention planning notes)

In DWR2 I used the ideas screen to present the list of objects practitioners identified in DWR 1. I began by facilitating the prioritisation of their objects:

…one of the exercises we did last week was to identify some of the objects that you thought, some of the areas you thought you were working on. There were quite a few, some of which could be said to be outcomes. So, what I want you to do is, to start off, is to look at these objects, and I've got them here and what I want you to do, perhaps in pairs, is to have a look at them. First discuss whether they are objects or outcomes. Then discuss how you might prioritise those objects.

DB - Do you want us to prioritise these? (picks up paper)

RCD – …first of all I want you to decide whether they are object or outcome. So, I always ask myself "What's to happen?" That's the outcome. "This isn't going to happen unless…" That's the object – the thing that's got to be shifted. See what I mean? So the question is 'Are these outcomes or objects?' Then after that, how would you go about prioritising the objects?

(DWR 2: Researcher (as facilitator) Video audio transcription)

Discussions were emotionally charged as practitioners questioned and sought clarification from each other as a way of expanding their learning through workshop discussions:

Ernest: (READS OUT AN OBJECT FROM THE LIST ON THE IDEAS SCREEN) *'Working on notions of masculinity'.*

Will: What do you mean by masculinity? In our group most of the men are what you would call 'men's men' you know? What that means I haven't got a bloody clue. Is it sort of a bloke who goes (makes gestures with his upper body of a 'lone rider' type of man moving)... Just be yourself, you know? Is that what we're talking about?

Ted: Masculinity tends to be very active. It tends to follow traits of other men. It tends be about being a provider, a protector. It tends to be a perceived image, whereas women...

Will: Men doing men's jobs. Is that what you mean?

Ted: Yeah, it could be jobs. It could be the way they behave. It could be the way they reason with things, so that if something happens to me, this is how I'll react.

Ernest: Yeah...we work with dads who go through an awful lot of turmoil and I think it's important for the group that there's a culture there that lets them not be ashamed to show that turmoil, so they don't have to put it under a lid, come in and carry on (imitates Will's earlier 'lone rider' man gesture)

(DWR 2: Researcher (as facilitator) Video audio transcription)

In the above extract, Will questioned the term 'masculinity', drawing practitioners' attention to culturally laden ideas about its characteristics, assisted through his arm gestures (in Figure 5.2 he was critically demonstrating an idea of being a man as 'macho'). In turn, other practitioners provided a more expanded perspective of what they meant by the term 'masculinity'. This eventually led to triggering the group to work on a collectively informed problem and potential object, the problem of whether and to what extent practitioners were consciously working on

Figure 5.2 An emotionally charged moment in the change laboratory. (Artwork by Brittany Molineux).

developing a group culture which challenged notions of what it is to be a male, in their respective father groups. In this kind of heated discussion, Virkkunen and Newnham (2013) provide useful advice for the researcher-interventionist:

> Such a course builds a shared recognition of a problem that needs to be solved and becomes the first stimulus of the participants' joint problem solving.
> The task of the researcher-interventionist is to turn the emotional involvement into propulsion of intellectual analysis by turning the discussion in the direction of the systemic causes of the problematic situation.
>
> (Virkkunen and Newnham 2013: 80)

- **Facilitating a 'transformation of the activity'**

In DWR workshop 3, I aimed to facilitate a 'transformation of the activity', by which I mean facilitating a new way of practitioners seeing their work.

Accordingly, I went back to previous DWR video data and ethnographic data from the father group observations and interviews and located data linked to the past and their connections with the present. Extracts of video clips for the mirror screen were therefore more deliberate by DWRs 3 and 4. I extracted video clips for contradictions, particularly between objects of the past and present and between objects and tools, to trigger dialectical movement for expansive learning:

> The dynamics of the expansive learning process in CL are created through the dialectical movement from one observation, interpretation or suggestion to another. These complement, but also compete and contradict each other. A contradiction between conceptualizations leads to a quest for an idea of an object or process that could mediate between the opposites. In the Change Laboratory, this process does not proceed primarily on the verbal level as a rhetorical process, but as an object-oriented inquiry, in which the ideas are anchored to data concerning the activity and a historical view of its development.
>
> The researcher-interventionist can use a variety of discursive tools and probes to support the dialectic movement of collective thinking from one view to another, opposing one, and to an expansive reconceptualization of the problem situation that makes the surpassing of the contradiction possible, by finding in the empirical reality a mediator for bridging the two opposing poles of the contradiction into a functioning whole.
>
> (Virkkunen and Newnham 2013: 113)

The task for DWR 3 was for them to start to consider the tools in relation to objects they were working on for father involvement, to identify whether there was a contradiction. Within our discussion I proposed the idea that relationships they developed historically could be used as a tool to work on current objects, and this led to an expanded discussion about the perimeters of using their relationships with group members (fathers), as a tool to move groups forward. They expanded ideas about appropriate conditions (rules in the AT diagram) for using existing relationships with the men/fathers, as a tool to move the group forward:

> RC-D (REFERS TO MIRROR SCREEN DATA) Right, so there's a bit of dispute going on, whether you can or you can't'… when I proposed the idea of, you using those relationships to then work on other things. What you were saying was, well yes we do, but sometimes that doesn't work; when that tool doesn't work, we have to go back, and that's a problem, you said.
> RC-D PLAYS VIDEO EXTRACT FROM PREVIOUS DWR ON THE MIRROR DATA SCREEN
> *Well I think quite often that you don't see people for quite a long time so you have, I mean one father turned up to see probably Pete and he didn't really realise Pete had gone. But something happened in his life where he wasn't able to attend anything for three or four months. And now he, he's back and he's done two weeks, um and he was intending to come regularly again. So I think their lives are complicated and therefore that relationship breaks down for a little while, and you have to rebuild it. And also you try and integrate new people into the group as well. So the group is never static. I think that's one of the issues* (MIRROR SCREEN VIDEO DATA).
> Ernest: That's really true. If you think about Andy who comes to the group, you remember Andy, there's been quite a lot of difficulty with some of the other dads we've had you know, in terms of accepting him. Which was quite hidden for a while but um, but it has shifted again hasn't it?
> RC-D: So that's almost two things, one is group dynamics, and the other is people coming and going and having to remake relationships. So do you think it's two issues then?
> Ernest: Yeah, yeah. They can be. I mean for example we've had another dad come in recently haven't we who's completely so different to all the rest of them. And we're surprised that he's coming back – he's a very middle class father, you know, um who spends his whole time with his children at the moment, um but he's opened up… I'm saying he's opened up new possibilities for the group in a way hasn't he?
> Anna: But I would think that was, that is about the relationship that you have, and trust that you have built up with them, that is then

Transformative visual representations 113

enabling you to move them up. It might not be on the agenda that you wanted, but in fact what you're probably achieving is safety for those children and support for those families to help them move on. So actually, if you weren't there, within a very short time it could degenerate into those children being taken into care or more serious relationships.

RC-D So the continuity of your relationship with fathers, i.e. if you weren't there, is that continuity an important 'rule', not just in terms of the group but in terms of you being there in order to work on other things with those fathers?

(DWR 3: Researcher (as facilitator) Video audio transcript)

Figure 5.3 provides a visual representation of part of the analysis in relation to the AT contextual diagram and how the process of change occurred from past to present to move respective groups forward, including conditions preventing them moving forward, which could be turned into potential objects. It illustrates how practitioners were working on a representation of their work activity through the CL intervention. The emerging contradiction depicted in Figure 5.3 is between rules and tools (discontinuity in attendance and built relationships). When this happened, a new object was needed to sustain group unity and then move the group forward. Practitioners agreed unity would not happen unless they developed a group culture, so that then became their object.

DWR 4 aimed to work on further contradictions, both within the object and between object and tool as we started to consider how they kept groups together through developing a group culture, and how they worked on developing father involvement (as they saw it), to enable better relationships with children. The main purposes for DWR 4 were:

- To get practitioners to question whether there are two objects they are working on (for the individual and for the group) with the outcome of father involvement
- To get the practitioners to identify a secondary contradiction i.e., tools and their appropriateness. Are they using the same tools for the individual and group? Can some tools work for many objects, or are different tools used for different objects. How are the tools different and why?

As discussions in CL sessions progressed, practitioners began to talk about further contradictions in their work. Whilst I will not go into the substantive issues in this methodological chapter, I will reveal how the final contradiction in this study lay in the groups themselves.

One of the main contradictions relating to their work was between the social identity associated with being part of the group and the individual

114 Transformative visual representations

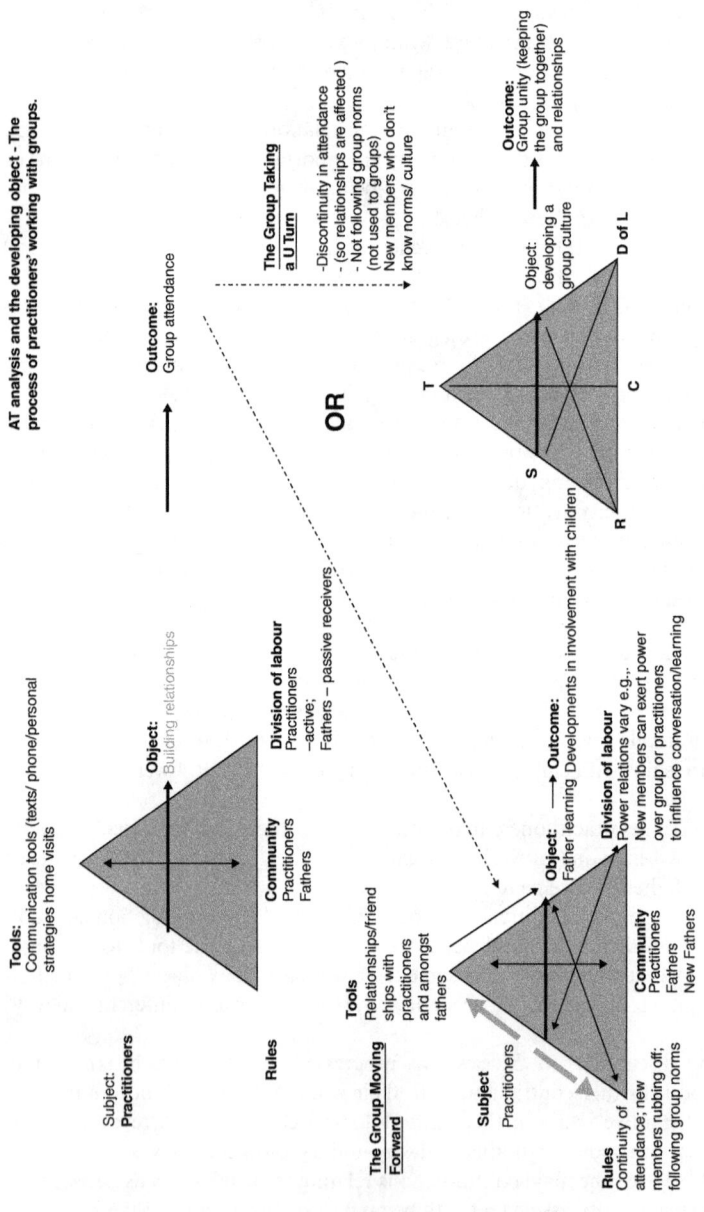

Figure 5.3 Activity theory analysis and the developing object – The process of practitioners' working with groups.

cultural meanings of masculinities with which the men arrived at the group. On the one hand, the characteristic conditions of most groups are about being a collective and talking things through; and on the other hand, fathers came to the groups with a 'lone rider' image of manhood. Contradictions were discussed to expand and clarify practitioners' understanding of issues they were working on 'as objects' with their respective father groups. For the practitioners, constructing a group culture as an 'object' of the group was a way to challenge how the men saw being male and fathering, for the purpose of sensitising the men within the groups, to reflect on what they did, with the outcome of better father–child relationships, as they saw it.

Methodological reflections and conclusion: the Change Lab. as a collaborative visual language of description

The chapter has demonstrated the part played by visual representations in CL. In the study, three screens were pivotal to using theory through CL methodology. As a visual representation, critiques of the AT diagram revolve around its oversimplification of theory. In response, Spinuzzi's (2020) discussion of Engeström's work as a form of participatory research design supported its usefulness as a visual heuristic. To this I also propose CL provides a collaborative visual language of description, in which:

> Engeström provided a graphical heuristic (the now-famous triangle) for picturing Leont'ev's activity system. This heuristic, which has been derided by some critics (e.g., Miller 2011), was meant not only as an analytical device for researchers but (critically) also as a way to communicate with – and codesign work with – research participants (e.g., Engeström 1999; Engeström and Sannino 2010). That is, it served as an interventionist "language game" (Ehn 1989) similar to …other participatory designers used to leverage the tacit expertise of participants. This point has been overlooked by those who have critiqued the triangle heuristic as an oversimplified theoretical tool (See Sannino 2011 for further elaboration of this point, and see Engeström 2018: 23 and 78 for other representations Engeström has developed for local stakeholders.)
>
> (Spinuzzi 2020: 10–11)

What I see is important about the AT diagram as a visual representation is how it addresses work activity as a context and simultaneously includes subjective understandings of context in which the participant is a part. Sometimes, the AT diagram raises questions to shed light on wider issues shaping context, or through which context shapes how the individual navigates their cultural world(s). I could see this in the study as I observed practitioners through their participation in engaging with the diagram,

116 Transformative visual representations

expanding their knowledge of fathers in relation to their cultural contexts of geography and class. This is a complex set of relationships, with layers of meaning, in which the AT diagram helped to provide a deeper understanding of practitioner work activity.

The Mirror data screen gave a space for practitioners to distance themselves from their experience, to reflect and respond, rather than react, and it developed collective understanding, as a participatory experience. As the interventionist facilitating their reflections, I had to ask myself questions about making selections for mirror data, selections which contradicted what they had also said, so the mirror data acted as a stimulus for expansive learning actions, for example, through questioning. The questioning process is an example of what happens as a result of mirror data acting as stimulus, for expansive learning:

> ...questioning means criticizing or rejecting some aspects of the accepted practice, plan or wisdom. It is not primarily distanced intellectual criticism, but reflects an alarming and emotionally involved observation or anticipation of something that is against the values and commitments of the actors...The action of questioning can be divided into three phases. It starts when someone points out something that seems to contradict the prevailing way of thinking and the current practice or plan. This typically arouses emotional energy and triggers a debate on the factuality and notability of the observation that is experienced as negative. Such an observation also upsets the involved individuals' mental equilibrium and initiates in them a process of experiencing, that is to say, an inner work to regain the temporarily lost mental equilibrium ....
> (Virkkunen and Newnham 2013: 81–82)

According to Virkkunen and Newnham (2013), the process might even lead to defending current practice, for example, with phrases such as 'that's actually unusual'

> However, the mental equilibrium can also be regained by preliminarily accepting the unpleasant observation and beginning to analyze the situation in order to better understand it and its background. Often both defense by moralizing and blaming, on the one hand, and analysis of the situation, on the other, take place as interacting aspects of the same discourse in the session.
> (Virkkunen and Newnham 2013: 82)

Finally, the ideas screen documented emerging ideas as they occurred through referring to the other screens. It demonstrated a practical and theoretical coherence in research practice through working with the other screens. Proponents about this methodological process sometimes refer to it as a cyclical process; critiques contest the idea (Augustsson 2021). My reflections as a researcher-interventionist suggest using the three screens in CL was neither cyclical nor linear as a mechanism of research design; but there was a coherence at work, ascending from the abstract to the concrete as a principle of expansive learning (Engeström 2020). I initially selected and used mirror data to conduct a historical reflection and analyses of practice to clarify context. I also used mirror data for empirical analyses and further historical analyses through discussion between myself and the practitioners. This methodological process of data collection, reflection and analysis created the stimulus for further development presented in an activity system diagram, as it shed light on new material in the ideas screen such as tool and object. It consequently formed a new model of their practice. In this respect the three screens provided a practical way of demonstrating coherence, so participants could collectively understand their work context through the AT diagram, ascending from the abstract diagram to their concrete interpretation of how their work happens in terms of certain processes through the AT diagram, and possibilities for transforming their work activity based on those insights. CL therefore offers a historically grounded account of how transformative collective practices produce and are produced through social interaction and human self(ves).

This chapter has demonstrated how practitioners can think about their work through visual representations. In this respect when we think about thinking, spatial thought is a valuable contribution to linguistic thought in CL methodology. Tversky (2019), for example, maintained the basis of abstract thinking is spatial thought, in which:

> Mental rotation is a distinctly visual-spatial transformation. It has been likened to watching something actually rotate in space...mental rotation task has become one of the major measures of spatial ability.
>
> (89–90)

And

> The ease of reasoning from well-designed diagrams has encouraged new fields to blossom, endeavors to make mathematics, logic, physics, and computer science diagrammatic, yet rigorous, in order to capitalize on our extraordinary abilities to see spatial relations and to reason about them. The rationale is the same, that diagrams use the power of spatial-motor reasoning for abstract reasoning.
>
> (2019: 210)

Given the main principles of CL involve a dynamic and systemic unit of analysis, 'activity', to understand practice and transform it through its lens, CL is an intervention which uses the visual to observe reasoning.

118 Transformative visual representations

Knowledge about practice is built up by what I call 'thinking through pictures'. The AT diagram constructs understanding about the relations which structure activity as context; reflecting on mirror data provides a stimulus to construct processes at work; and the ideas screen constructs possibilities for transforming the activity context, to address work-based problems. In this respect CL uses the three screens as visual representations transformatively, by combining the study of social context, process and change, and in doing so practitioners come to construct an understanding and transformative potential of their work activity, collectively, by thinking through pictures.

Notes

1. Sure Start was a UK poverty alleviation strategy for children and families under the age of 4, brought in by Tony Blair's Labour government between 1997 and 2007. Successive UK governments minimised its use through subsequent funding cuts and closures of Sure Start centres, replacing them with children centres, many of which sourced their own support for children's services.
2. See Blunden (2015) for a critique of Engeström's interpretation of CHAT and the unit of analysis.
3. Vygotsky, Leont'ev and Engeström are cited as key theorists in the development of CHAT, sometimes associated, respectively, with several generations of how mediation works; with Engeström (1987/2015, 1996a/1996b) developing an interventionist methodology CL, subsumed under 'Development Work Research' (DWR) and based on Leont'ev's idea of activity as a systemic mediational activity.
4. Dialectic here is taken from the Hegelian view of intellectual development in human history.
5. Langemeyer and Roth (2006) usefully and critically discuss the challenges for researchers interpreting Engeström's model as a dialectical social science.
6. The concept of shift of motive towards goal was introduced into activity theory by A.N. Leont'ev (1978) as a mechanism in the development of activity and personality. It describes what is happening 'when someone starts to perform certain actions under the influence of one motive but then continues to perform them for their own sake, because the motive has as it were shifted towards the goal' (302).

6 Conclusion

In the introduction I proposed the question 'how do social science researchers use visual technology to work on research problems in education, and what possibilities are available for educational ethnography?' I had two main aims and three objectives for this book. First, to position the use of visual technology in research designs so it is theoretically linked to educational problems. Second, to present a book with research designs using the visual in ways which are practically useful in a range of educational contexts. With the two aims in mind, I began to engage with writing about developing ethnographic research in education that includes visual and digital modes. In the book I focus on illustrating how I used visual technology in the form of digital video film and photographs, and I demonstrate how as a source of data, visual technology has potential in addressing educational problems and developing ethnographic knowledge, in a range of educational contexts.

Specifically, in Chapter 1, I set out the objectives for the book as:

1 Introducing philosophical positions underpinning the use of visual generally, to address educational problems and develop ethnographic knowledge in education.
2 Explicating the relationship between problem and theory in research designs using visual technology as a source of data in ethnographic oriented studies, drawing on project material.
3 Reflecting on the potential of using visual technology critically as a reflexive and dialectic source in producing ethnographic oriented studies in a range of educational contexts.

Chapter 2 'Visual Technology for Educational Ethnography' laid out the often-missed range of epistemological and ontological considerations in visual research. I discussed three philosophical positions: scientific realism, reflexivity and dialectics, as applied to visual-based research in social science literature. In the chapter, I referred to representations of reality and the visual as a way of introducing the three ontological and epistemological positions; but it is possible to take this further into broader fields of semiotics and post-human notions of reality. Gunther Kress (2010), for example, was instrumental in the development of a social semiotic theory of multimodality, of which visual communication is a part. Essentially in the idea of multimodality, Kress argued for a more inclusive form of communication, where we recognise how different modes of communication relate to one another, whether they are speech, image, moving pictures or writing. His concern was primarily language, but for Kress (2010) concepts like 'language' in conventional terms are 'not a big enough receptacle for all the semiotic stuff we ... could pour into it' (15). His social semiotic theory can be seen as a theory based on meaning, social context and cultural context; and he used that as a basis for thinking about multimodality, a phenomenon he equates with understanding the modes of communication (Armfield 2011). So, for example, in considering 'meaning', he cited the example of a sign directing customers into a supermarket car park, arguing, we derive its meaning, by the different semiotic modes it uses and how they work together – in this case, it is writing, image and colour. In the example of the car park sign, each mode performs a different function in terms of its semiotic work and therefore has different potentials for meaning. Kress (2010) therefore argued that a social theory of communication requires a multimodal explanation. The part 'social' plays is essential to his theory, because it is we who reproduce the sign by giving it meaning, and in doing so, we shape its meaning. In relation to digital technologies he argued for an expansion of traditional linguistic frames, into a semiotic frame which recognises the visual. For Kress (Kress and Burn 2005: 97), the place of linguistic thought, has to be rethought, so all aspects of representation are taken into account. In this respect he proposed the semiotic take says, 'pay attention to everything that is there', where the linguistic take says 'pay attention to features of language' (Kress and Burn 2005: 98). The frame becomes wider, opening possibilities and potential, for new ways of knowing, and therefore the kind of knowledge claims we can make as researchers researching educational problems. Speaking of the balance between the visual against the general multi-modal spectrum, Kress (2003) likened speech to video as a fluid visual modality, sitting against the less fluid and dynamic modes of writing and still images. He referred to such modes as resources, spatially and temporally organised, proposing:

> ...the possibilities that they provide the individual user for being agentive. In speech you can be agentive: you can shape to your needs much more than you can shape writing.
>
> (Kress 2003: 103–104)

Conclusion 121

Speaking with foresight in the move towards greater technology he portrayed and predicted the kinds of complexity with which we might be working with visual technology in the future:

> The screen or book will continue, but their relation to modes will change...we need to think separately about the three cultural technologies of communication: that of representation, that of production and that of dissemination, because they are always independently variable and always brought into conjunction.
>
> (Kress 2003: 104–105)

The idea of cultural technologies of communication; how they are represented, produced and disseminated is a huge step forward from Chapter 2's use of film and photography, which aimed understand the culture of anganwadi settings in Mumbai by examining the visual (as semiotic means) which make up cultures of pre-school slum settings, through the lens of the structure of pedagogic communication. The latter as a theory of communication depended mainly on action and direction, rather than interaction. Kress (2012) presented an alternative of how we might look at images, not as in communication, not as actions, but as capturing instances of interaction and communication; where the result is the existence, even for a moment, of 'community' (372). His is a social semiotic perspective, in which interaction became the basis both of meaning making (rather than a notion of meaning transfer) around similar experiences. ...and the meanings made in that interaction (...are) also the beginning of a store of shared cultural 'resources', sufficiently similarly understood to permit new interaction based on the present understanding of these 'shared resources' (Kress 2012: 372).

Certainly, the use of video technologies and video methodologies has allowed me to capture instances of interaction and how we resource those moments and by extension lays open potentials for human development, through communication.

The case study in Chapter 4, for example, demonstrated how digital video observation and computer editing (aspects of representation and production) make it possible to examine how opportunities for learning and development occur from the perspective of human development in cultural-historical psychology. This is because visual technologies can capture the complexity and dynamics of the material conditions and social expectations that make up a social situation of development, in a moment. In this respect, using visual technologies is a way of capturing instances of opportunities for development without being dependent on the temporal, because it can observe and capture the dialectic process. The study in Chapter 4 outlined how the research design incorporated video modalities of extraction and reflection, where both dialectic and reflexive ontological positions were combined for different purposes of the research design. The visual technologies themselves presented an opportunity to look at the social and material conditions through which the child's object-oriented motive emerged. The research team used video to extract the dialectic conditions of development and make the unconscious visible and, in doing so, provided a space to explore how opportunities for development were occurring through interactions. We used video in its reflective modality to take account of its reflexive quality, one that forms a connection between the observer and the subject of the image, a connection that turns back on the observer and affects how they see what they see and their interpretation:

> As the observer views an image, how they perceive it changes, because of shifts in perspective both physical and cognitive, directly brought about by the act of observation.
>
> (Haw and Hadfield 201: 50)

Of course, a sensitive downside to what we considered to be an exercise in 'making the unconscious, conscious' is that young children (or indeed vulnerable participants in general) might not recognise the process as one of exposing themselves when giving their 'informed consent' to participation the research. Field observation notes (text) do not actually manage to reflexively capture what I, as a researcher, felt at the time, as I tried to relay how I felt when I looked at the young child's face. In that moment, I saw both her actions and emotions at work, when writing 'Bea's expression changes, she is about to cry, as she stares at the reflection of herself being played back on the screen in front of her'. Looking reflexively from Bea's perspective, a closeup of the film captured a moment before the subject (Bea, a child, in the film extract) turned into an object (Bea, the child, seeing her face from the outside, as the 'other' in one sense). So, I maintain, whilst video has the power to elicit a response which is entirely different to that aroused by text, it has ethical significance for using it for reflection with potentially vulnerable social groups. Levinas (1999) wrote about facial expressions as ethical significance, where 'the face signifies the revelation of the other' (Levinas 1999: 171). For Levinas (1992) it also signified fragility and vulnerability of the 'other' and the need to protect, which we see in my recorded field notes about how family members surrounding Bea responded in that moment of sensitive drama. For researchers, I would maintain it is also a reminder of a researcher's personal responsibility for the 'other', when asking potentially vulnerable participants to reflect on themselves through film and video.

There were also pragmatic of reasons of course for using video methodology rather than observation in the child/human development study,

Conclusion   123

Figure 6.1 Image of international team – negotiation, collaboration and critique of model through shared video footage viewing.

particularly relevant to international research teams. First, it captures a detailed representation of an observable phenomena, which, as an international team, we viewed in our own contexts after the fieldwork period. Later, we gathered as a team on a digital platform and discussed our thoughts, whilst simultaneously viewing synchronised audio and video footage, alongside a digitised diagram of a developing model with which we were working.

Second, it was also possible to repeatedly analyse the footage in detail with scholars from varied international contexts because video is open to more detailed analysis compared to direct observation. Finally, it was possible to look at detail not only through patterns of social interaction but though the nuances of facial expressions and in this respect film and video have the unique capacity to realise the power of facial expressions to communicate.

The chapter concluded by reflecting on the value of both video modalities (extraction and reflection) and practical implications for social science researchers interested in using video to research child development and the child's perspective, particularly in relation to projects connected to identifying and promoting learner agency from a more psychological, rather than solely sociological perspective of agency. For educationalists, I believe the psychological addition sharpens our understanding of learning, learners and human development, whether our concern is children or adults.

The final study in the book (Chapter 5) used a combination of visual representations whose sources were essentially digital diagrams, video and display screens, to demonstrate how visual representations can work together in an interventionist, participatory research design, specifically

CL, to shed light on context, process and change as part of understanding professional development. This occurred through a transformative process of 'thinking through pictures'. By participatory I mean conducting research where all individuals involved are active participants in one or all the following – designing the project, identifying the research questions, carrying it out, analysing and writing up the research. In this respect participants can be co-investigators, co-analysis or co-writers, or all of the above. As an educational ethnographer, I have a history of using ethnographic techniques of participant observation and informal interviews to conduct research with children, parents, teachers and head teachers in home and school settings. Therefore, ethnographic-oriented research has and continues to provide me with a deep understanding of childhood and schooling. However, my interest in DWR with practitioners stemmed from a desire to go beyond deep understanding; I wanted to weave in change; and in doing so, bridge research with development. DWR methodology, combined with its strong philosophical, theoretical and practical basis, allowed me to address this purpose.

Chapter 5 and DWR methodology demonstrated a dialectical ontological position on reality in its interventionist approach from a cultural historical perspective. Here the unit of analysis was 'activity', and a digitally produced heuristic diagram represented on one of three screens allowed practitioners to conceptualise their work activity with the aim of expanding practitioners' understanding of their work through a systemic approach. At the same time practitioners learnt how contradictions within a system propel possibilities for change, and in this respect, a dialectical[1] mechanism is at work, driving change.

From a social semiotics perspective and view of image discussions, the visual representations in CL prompted instances of interaction, but the diagram, and identifying the 'object' as it related to the diagram, prompted a different interaction to the energetic discussions provoked by contradictory messages presented in mirror data. In both instances we can say semiotic processes were at work. Reflecting on a sketch (drawing) made by two surgeons prior to an operation which they were about to perform, Kress (2012) stated 'It is an instance of communication in which new meanings were made; that is, in which the meaning-resource of the sketch became the prompt for interpretations, and, in that, re-made resources in that community' (374). The AT diagram was designed by Engeström to work with a group of practitioners and in doing so constitutes a mode in that it is 'a socially shaped and culturally driven semiotic resource for meaning making' (Kress 2010: 79). Resources and community in DWR methodology are about joint knowledge and meaning being created through an interacting group of practitioners, interacting and resourcing the three visual representations. This could resemble what the visual social anthropologist, Banks, would possibly count as a third kind of visual record, the 'collaborative representation' (Banks 1995) (the first two being pre-existing visual representations used by researchers and the second being participant-produced visual representations). Alternatively, I propose DWR, when combined with ethnographic oriented methods, constitutes another kind of visual record, a fourth kind, 'the transformative visual representation', because as an intervention, it can transform how practitioners are able to view their work activity and its potentials and possibilities.

In the final part of the book, I would like to draw on some of the insights for the future I have gained from different perspectives, about using the visual in and for educational research, given the new possibilities of production through visual technology. There are, I believe, key issues for learning and knowledge emerging if we assume that knowledge has to be realised in some form for it to exist (Kress in Bearne 2005: 291):

> ... new technologies allow you to configure, to materialize, to realize knowledge according to your interests, and according to the interests which you as a rhetor imagine your audience has, the question of how knowledge is configured and constantly reconfigured becomes really important because the learner engages with knowledge in a particular configuration, either written, or in image form, or in a teacher's gesture, as a teacher demonstrates. The way that bit of the world is configured, materialized, sets the ground on which the learner engages with it, it shapes the learner's learning.
>
> (Kress in Bearne 2005)

Kress provided an insightful hypothetical example of a physics lesson in which he compared a learner learning about states of matter from a classic diagram in a textbook, to watching a moving image in which:

> You show a glass vessel on the Bunsen burner, a block of ice is in there as the solid, the Bunsen burner is lit and something happens to the block of ice: bubbles come up. Now the question for the student is, what are these bubbles? Are they the molecules that are freeing themselves or are they something else? Whole new questions arise, through a shift which is brought about by a different form of representation.
>
> (ibid.)

Kress's example raises epistemological questions about how and whose knowledge is created and represented when representations change and '...how this epistemological change has an effect on the person who engages with it' (Kress in Bearne 2005: 291).

Moss (2013) observed how practitioner researchers are increasingly interested in the potentials of new technologies and promise of visual research methods, and this will equally apply to educational practitioners

Conclusion

who are also researching educational problems. She warned researchers about the need to weigh up various respective forms of analysis which can occur when image and text are used together and alone. Despite warnings about analysis, however, Moss' (2013) generally optimistic approach to our curiosities as educational researchers takes us forward, in that...

> Researchers in education like other members of the wider social science community, 'epitomise the visual culture that they also inhabit'... To wonder how we might refine our research approaches in the future, to see social change, and to be troubled by it; to better understand the unconscious and conscious forms of the visual, and what can be asked of this data in between the social and the technological and in between difference and indifference; these are new questions for educational researchers...
>
> (Moss 2013: 75)

Pink (2021) also ushers in thoughts for future research, advocating a 'futures-oriented' approach to ethnographic practice and the reflexive, ethical and interventional responsibilities this brings, whilst also accounting theoretically and practically for our digital and emerging intelligent environments (24). For me this raises questions about the role of theory and the extent to which it changes as we engage with visual representations as part of our world, not as researchers collecting visual data, but rather on how people experience, learn and know through the visual. These are questions from a more phenomenological position, which go beyond representations to how we are shaped and shape our society, its learning and learners as part of its visual culture, and the social, semiotic and epistemological effects of students engaging with new technologies.

Pink (2021) proposed the idea of a 'digital wayfarer', in which we weave through our contemporary digital material environment, through, for example, creating and sharing camera-phone images whilst in movement (Pink and Hjorth 2014). To understand the ways digital and material are increasingly in relation with one another, in a continuous process of development and change, Pink et al. (2016) developed the concept of 'digital materiality', where:

> ...things and processes in which digital and material qualities are entangled, and in which the material does not necessarily precede the digital.
>
> (43)

The idea of our being in movement with our technologies, images and image making, in which our online and offline worlds are intertwined as part of the digital materiality, resonates with increasing scholarship subsumed under the new materialist ontology (and there are several new materialisms), often characterised as post-humanist in perspective. Here the term 'post' ... 'decentres the human, to posit a world in which humans are not the only or most important agents' (c.f. Pennycook 2018 in Toohey and Smythe 2022: 123). Instead, we as humans are a part of a wider relational existence, where everything is connected and in constant motion. In general, a relational non-dualistic (for example, between natural and social worlds) characteristic is associated with post-human new materialism, within which is a notion of movement, with scholars using concepts such as assemblage (c.f. Deleuze and Guattari 1987 in Toohey and Smythe 2022: 127). In such a framework of reality, humans continuously modify their environment by being part of it with often uncertain and I would say, by implication, unintentional outcomes. Here, 'humans and materials are seen as forming unpredictable and shifting assemblages constituted by a multiplicity of vital things...which together create phenomena under investigation' (Dagenais et al, cited in Toohey and Smythe 2022: ibid.). Taking this characteristic into areas of education, schooling and the curriculum, for example, Toohey and Smythe (2022) concern themselves with educational problems in teacher education with EAL learners and its response to difference (as diversity) in terms of race, class, gender, language, ethnicity and religion, which have become defining features of many contemporary classrooms. In such classrooms we might assume, from a post-human perspective, diversity is being constructed through constant changing relations or connections, which Toohey and Smythe (2022) suggest may give rise to new problems and new concepts. From a researcher's perspective, Denzin et al. (2023) also propose qualitative research is actually in a new space, a starting point for a new beginning (p. 647), living through the traumatic effects of a global pandemic. My feeling is that effects are defined and redefined by schools, teachers, pupils and parents and with it has come what Denzin and Lincoln (2023) call 'a new language of living, a post pandemic pedagogy of new terms and practices' (647), filtered from experiences since 2020. In this transformative post-pandemic 'contested future' (ibid.) they say we are evolving, insist we be hopeful, and at the same time, as researchers, ask us to provide new narratives in this transitional moment (652–653). This is no easy mission. Certainly, the complexity of contemporary classrooms as we increasingly see them becoming digitally material educational environments will raise both curiosity-driven research questions and ethical issues. Such complexity, as I see it, reflects some similarity to the complexity raised in Kress's (2010) notion of multimodality, alongside a notion of educational encounters and pedagogy in classrooms that is understood in more relational ways, in which:

> With the recognition that multimodality...occur in shifting assemblages of 'other discourses, peoples, beings, languages (that we know and do not yet know) and things', we can see a wider semiotic

landscape ... a more activity-oriented, spontaneously creative and processual notion of how it is that meanings are made.

(Toohey and Smythe 2022: 127)

If visual ethnographers are, as Pink (2021) maintained, at a turning point within the current fourth industrial revolution characterised by new technologies impacting and even challenging what it is to be human, then she also suggested we consider the future in terms of new kinds of connections, stating ...

> We should take account for how the technological possibilities signified by new modes of automation and connectedness and the merging of things and processes of different kinds will create new subject matter, new image making and sharing technologies and new ways of connecting with and engaging with others, as both academic and applied ethnographers.
>
> (32)

Pink (2021) proposed the anthropology of emerging technologies is critical in terms of the impact of the fourth industrial revolution, where questions of why we need technology and what do we do with it are more important than assuming technology has an impact and brings about change. This future technology approach is non predicative, instead asking how technology will become part of the human existence. It will inevitably raise questions about how we might evolve our use of visual technology as educational ethnographers. In photography, for example, Pink (2021) suggested we might consider how devices are used in material and social environments, which impacts the composition of images and the experiences of using them. These are epistemological related questions about knowledge construction through relations between visual technology, cultural, social and material contexts.

In using ethnographic-oriented research in education combined with visual technology I have a growing awareness of the multiple ways we can come to know and understand what it is to be a learner through visual technology, as both an affective and cognitive experience. The research studies and philosophy and practice discussed in the book to address educational problems do, I hope, hold scope for contributing to research designs using the visual where relationships between problem, theory and visual technology remain key questions to consider. I hope the book also raises awareness about the potential of visual technology as a reflexive and dialectical source in producing ethnographic-oriented knowledge, raising new questions for researchers in a range of educational and social science contexts, with our increasingly digitised material educational environments. In this respect, future methodological questions for educational problems are not only about how we use visual technology for educational ethnography but also about how those involved in educational settings evolve through technology and how this creates new pedagogic cultures and routes to knowing more about the experience of and for education through the visual.

Note

1 Dialectic here is taken from the Hegelian sense of transformations in human consciousness.

Appendix 1
Examples of educational ethnographies

> Ethnography has become one of the major methods of researching educational settings. Its key strength is its emphasis on understanding the perceptions and cultures of the people and organizations studied. Through prolonged involvement with those who are being studied, the ethnographic researcher is able gradually to enter their world and gain an understanding of their lives.
>
> [Walford, G. (2004) "PREFACE", Troman, G., Jeffrey, B. and Walford, G. (Ed.) *Identity, Agency and Social Institutions in Educational Ethnography* (*Studies in Educational Ethnography, Vol. 10*), Emerald Group Publishing Limited, Bingley, p. VII.]

Aggleton, P. (1987) *Rebels without a Cause? Middle Class Youth and the Transition from School to Work.* London: Falmer Press.

Awad, S. (2015) *An Ethnographic Study of the Ways in Which Faith is Manifested in Two Primary Schools* (PhD Thesis Liverpool John Moores University).

Ball, S. J. (1981) *Beachside Comprehensive: A Case Study of Schooling.* Cambridge: Cambridge University Press.

Bhatti, G. (1999) *Asian Children at Home and at School: An Ethnographic Study.* London: Routledge.

Brooker, L. (2002) *Starting School: Young Children Learning Cultures.* Buckingham: Open University Press.

Burgess, R. G. (2018) *Experiencing Comprehensive Education: A Study of Bishop McGregor School.* (Reprint) London: Routledge.

Chawla-Duggan, R. (2007) *Children's Learner Identity as Key to Quality Education: Eight Case Studies of Schooling in India.* Lewiston, New York: Edwin Mellen Press.

Connolly, P. (1998) *Racism, Gender Identities and Young Children.* London: Routledge.

Corrigan, P. (1979) *Schooling the Smash Street Kids.* London: Macmillan.

Delamont, S. ([1976] 2018 e-book) *Interaction in the Classroom.* London: Routledge.

Delamont, S. ([1980] 1990) *Sex Roles and the School.* London: Routledge.

Delamont, S., and Galton, M. ([1986] 2014) *Inside the Secondary Classroom.* London: Routledge and Kegan Paul.

Davies, B. ([1993] 2003) *Shards of Glass: Children Reading and Writing Beyond Gendered Identities.* Cresskill: Hampton Press.

Denscombe, M. (1985) *Classroom Control: A Sociological Perspective.* London: George Allen and Unwin.

Appendix 1 131

Foley, D. E. ([1990] 2010) *Learning Capitalist Culture*. Philadelphia: University of Pennsylvania Press.

Fordham, S. (1996) *Blacked Out: Dilemmas of Race, Identity, and Success in Capital High*. Chicago: University of Chicago Press.

Hargreaves, D. ([1967] 2011) *Social Relations in Secondary School*. London: Routledge and Kegan Paul.

Hargreaves, D., Hester, S., and Mellor, F. (1975) *Deviance in Classrooms*. London: Routledge and Kegan Paul.

Heath, Shirley Brice (1983) *Ways with Words: Language, Life, and Work in Communities and Classrooms*. New York: Cambridge University Press.

Hemmings, A. (1998) "The Self-Transformations of African American Achievers." *Youth & Society* 29 (1998): 330–368.

Holland, Dorothy C., and Eisenhart, Margaret A. (1990) *Educated in Romance: Women, Achievement, and College Culture*. Chicago: University of Chicago Press.

Jackson, P. ([1968] 1991) *Life in Classrooms*. New York: Holt, Rinehart & Winston.

Lacey, C. (1970) *Hightown Grammar*. Manchester: Manchester University Press.

Mac an Ghaill, Maírtín (1994) *The Making of Men*. Buckingham: Open University Press.

McLaren, P. (1986) *Schooling as a Ritual Performance*. London: Routledge and Kegan Paul.

Mizra, H.S. (1992) *Young, Female and Black*. London: Routledge.

Pollard, A. (1985) *The Social World of the Primary School* London, Holt, Rinehart & Winston.

Filer, A. and Pollard, A. (2000) *The Social World of Pupil Assessment*. London: Holt, Rinehart and Winston.

Sewell, T. (1997) *Black Masculinities and Schooling: How Black Boys Survive Modern Schooling*. Staffordshire, England: Trentham Books.

Thorne, Barrie (1993) *Gender Play: Girls and Boys in Schools*. Buckingham: Open University.

Walford, G. (1986) *Life in Public Schools*, London, Methuen; Published in 2014 by Routledge.

Willis, P. (1977) *Learning to Labour: How Working-Class Kids Get Working Class Jobs*. Farnborough: Saxon House. Reprint by Columbia University Press (1 Dec. 1981).

Wolcott, H. (1973/2003) *The Man in the Principal's office: An ethnography*. Walnut Creek, CA: AltaMira Press.

Woods, P. ([1979] 2012) *The Divided School*. London: Routledge and Kegan Paul. Reprinted in 2012.

References

Alexander, R. 2001. *Culture and pedagogy: International comparisons in primary education*. Oxford: Blackwell.
Andy, Hargreaves. [1967] 2011. *Social relations in secondary school*. London: Routledge and Kegan Paul.
Atkinson, P. 1985. *Language, structure and reproduction: An introduction to the sociology of Basil Bernstein*. London: Methuen.
Augustsson, D. 2021. Expansive learning in a change laboratory intervention for teachers. *Journal of Educational Change*, 22(4), 475–499.
Armfield, D. (2011). Multimodality: A Social Semiotic Approach to Contemporary Communication. *Technical Communication Quarterly*, 20(3), 347–349.
Banks, M. 1995. Visual research methods. *Social Research Update*, 11. [Online]. Available from: http://sru.soc.surrey.ac.uk/SRU11/SRU11.html
Banks, M. 2001. *Visual methods in social research*. London: SAGE.
Banks, M. 2007. *Using visual data in qualitative research*. London: SAGE.
Banks, M. and Zeitlyn, D. 2015. *Visual methods in social research*. 2nd ed. SAGE.
Barrett, B. 2014. Bernstein in the urban classroom: A case study. Paper presented at the Eighth International Basil Bernstein Symposium on Sociology of Education, Nanzan University, Nagoya, Japan, July 9–12.
Barry, D. 1994. Making the invisible visible: Using analogically-based methods to surface unconscious organizational processes. *Organization Development Journal*, 12, 37–48.
Bassey, M. 1999. *Case study research in educational settings*. Buckingham: Open University Press.
Bateson, G. and Mead, M. 1942. *Balinese character: A photographic analysis*. New York: Academy of Sciences.
Baxter, L. A. and Montgomery, B. M. 1996. *Relating: Dialogues and dialectics*. New York: Guilford.
Beach, Dennis, Bagley, Carl and Silva, Sofia Marques Da. 2018. *The Wiley handbook of ethnography of education*. Hoboken, NJ: John Wiley & Sons.
Bearne, E. 2005. Interview with Gunther Kress. *Discourse: Studies in the Cultural Politics of Education*, 26(3), 287–299.
Becker, H. S. 1974. Photography and sociology. *Studies in Visual Communication*, 1(1), 3–26. Available from: https://repository.upenn.edu/svc/vol1/iss1/3
Béhague, D. P., Kanhonou, L. G., Filippi, V., Lègonou, S. and Ronsmans, C. 2008. Pierre Bourdieu and transformative agency: A study of how patients in Benin

negotiate blame and accountability in the context of severe obstetric events. *Sociology of Health and Illness*, 30(4), 489–510.
Berger, J. 1972. *Ways of seeing*. London: BBC Penguin.
Bernstein, B. 1971. *Class, codes and control. Vol.1, Theoretical studies towards a sociology of language*. London: Routledge and Kegan Paul.
Bernstein, B. 1975. *Class, codes and control. Vol. 3, Towards a theory of educational transmissions*. London: Routledge & Kegan Paul.
Bernstein, B. 1990/2003. *Class, codes and control. Vol. 4, The structuring of pedagogic discourse*. London: Routledge.
Bernstein, B. 2000. *Pedagogy. Symbolic control and identity: Theory, research, critique*. Lanham: Rowman & Littlefield Publishers.
Blunden, A. 2010. *An interdisciplinary theory of activity*. Boston, MA: Brill.
Blunden, A. 2015. *Engeström's activity theory and social theory* [Online]. Available from: *Andy Blunden's Writings* ethicalpolitics.org
Buckingham, D. 2009. Creative visual methods in media research: Possibilities, problems and proposals. *Media, Culture and Society*, 31, 559–577.
Burgess, R. G. 1982/2015. *Field research: A sourcebook and field manual*. London: Routledge.
Burgess, R. G. 1984. *In the field: An introduction to field research*. 1st ed. London: Routledge.
Chawla-Duggan, R. 2007. *Children's learner identity as key to quality primary education: Eight case studies of schooling in India Today*. Lewiston, New York: The Edwin Mellen Press.
Chawla-Duggan, R. and Konantambigi, R. 2022. Crisis as microgenetic developmental transitions: Using explorative activities in micro-transitions to recognize opportunities for development between young children and their fathers – A cross-national study. In: M. Fleer, M. Hedegaard, E. Ødegaard and H. V. Sørensen, eds. *Qualitative studies of exploration in childhood education: Cultures of play and learning in transition*. London: Bloomsbury Academic, pp. 117–146.
Chawla-Duggan, R., Konantambigi, R., Lam, M. and Sollied, S. 2022. Double stimulation and transformative agency through video modalities with young children: A cross-national study of pedagogic relationships in families. *Pedagogy, Culture and Society*, 30(1), 89–109.
Christensen, P. and James. A. 2008. *Research with children: Perspectives and practices*. London: Routledge.
Clark, A. 2005. 'The silent voice of the camera?' Young children and photography as a tool for listening. *Early Childhood Folio*, 9, 28–33.
Clark, A. 2007. A hundred ways of listening. Gathering children's perspective of their early childhood environment. *Young Children*, 62(3), 76–81.
Clark, A. and Moss, P. 2011. *Listening to young children: The mosaic approach*. 2nd ed. London: National Children's Bureau and Joseph Rowntree Foundation.
Clifford, J. 1986. Introduction: Partial truths. In: J. Clifford and G. Marcus, eds. *Writing culture the poetics and politics of ethnography*. Berkeley CA: University of California Press.
Cochran-Smith, M. and Lytle, S. L. 2009. *Inquiry as stance: Practitioner research for the next generation*. New York, NY: Teachers College Press.
Cohen, A. P. and Rapport, N. 1995. *Questions of consciousness*. London: Routledge.

References

Cole, M. and Engeström, Y. 1993. A cultural-historical approach to distributed cognition. In: G. Salomon, ed. *Distributed cognitions: Psychological and educational considerations*. New York, NY: Cambridge University Press, pp. 1–46.

Cole, M. and Engeström, Y. 2007. Cultural-historical approaches to designing for development. In: J. Valsiner and A. Rosa, eds. *The Cambridge handbook of sociocultural psychology*. New York: Cambridge University Press, pp. 484–507.

Collier, J. and Collier, M. 1986. *Visual Anthropology: Photography as a research method* (Revised). University of New Mexico Press.

Collier, J. C., Jr. 1967. *Visual anthropology: Photography as a research method*. New York: Holt, Rinehart and Winston.

Daniels, H. 1989. Visual displays as tacit relays of the structure of pedagogic practice. *British Journal of the Sociology of Education*, 10 (2), 123–140.

Daniels, H. 2001. *Vygotsky and pedagogy*. London; New York: Routledge Falmer.

Daniels, H., Thompson, I., Tse, H. M. and Porter, J. 2022. Learning lessons from the collaborative design of guidance for new build schools. *European Educational Research Journal*, 21(4), 585–601. https://doi.org/10.1177/14749041221080892

Datta, V. 2001. *A study of urban early childhood programmes*. (Report sponsored by UNICEF).

Datta, V. 2005. Reaching the unreached: Early childhood care and education intervention in India. In: J. Patnaik, ed. *Children in South Asia: A critical look at issues, policies and programmes*. Greenwich: C.T. Information age publishing, pp. 88–112.

Delamont, S. 2009. The only honest thing: Autoethnography, reflexivity and small crises in fieldwork. *Ethnography and Education*, 4(1), 51–63.

Denzin, N. K. and Lincoln, Y. S. 2005. The discipline and practice of qualitative research. In: N. K. Denzin and Y. S. Lincoln, eds. *The Sage handbook of qualitative research*. 3rd ed. Thousand Oaks, CA: SAGE, pp. 1–32.

Denzin, N. K. and Lincoln, Y. S. 2023. *The SAGE handbook of qualitative research*. 6th ed. London: SAGE.

Donnelly, M. 2016. *Framing the geographies of higher education participation: Schools, place and national identity*, Vol. 42. Wiley-Blackwell. Available from: https://doi.org/10.1002/berj.3196

Dreze, J. 2006. Universalisation with quality, ICDS in a rights perspective. *The Economic and Political Weekly*, 45(34), 3706–3715.

Ehn, P. (1989). *Work-oriented design of computer artifacts*. Hillsdale: Lawrence Erlbaum Associates.

Engeström, Y. 1987/2015. *Learning by expanding. An activity-theoretical approach to developmental research*. New York, NY: Cambridge University Press.

Engeström, Y. 1996a. Development as breaking away and opening up: A challenge to Vygotsky and Piaget. *Swiss Journal of Psychology*, 55, 126–132.

Engeström, Y. 1996b. Developmental work research as educational research: Looking ten years back and into the zone of proximal development. *Nordisk Pedagogik*, 16, 131–143.

Engeström, Y. 1999. Innovative learning in work teams: Analysing cycles of knowledge creation in practice. In: Y. Engeström, R. Miettinen and R. L. Punamaki, eds. *Perspectives on activity theory*. Cambridge: Cambridge University Press, pp. 377–406.

Engeström, Y. 2007. Putting activity theory to work: The change laboratory as an application of double stimulation. In: H. Daniels, M. Cole and J. V. Wertsch, eds.

References 135

The Cambridge companion to Vygotsky. Cambridge: Cambridge University Press, pp. 363–382.
Engeström, Y. 2008. *From teams to knots: Activity-theoretical studies of collaboration and learning at work*. New York, NY: Cambridge University Press.
Engeström, Y. 2018. *Expertise in transition: Expansive learning in medical work*. New York, NY: Cambridge University Press.
Engeström, Y. 2020. Ascending from the abstract to the concrete as a principle of expansive learning. *Psychological Science and Education*, 25(5), 31–43.
Engeström, Y., Lompscher, J. and Rückriem, G., eds. 2005. *Putting activity theory to work: Contributions from developmental work research*. Berlin: Lehmanns Media.
Engeström, Y. and Sannino, A. 2010. Studies of expansive learning: Foundations, findings and future challenges. *Educational Research Review*, 5(1), 1–24.
Engeström, Y., Virkkunen, J., Helle, M., Pihlaja, J. and Poikela, R. 1996. The change laboratory as a tool for transforming work. *Lifelong learning in Europe*, 1(2), 10–17.
Englund, C. and Price, L. 2018. Facilitating agency: The change laboratory as an intervention for collaborative sustainable development in higher education. *International Journal for Academic Development*, 23(3), 192–205.
Erickson, F. 2011. Uses of video in social research: A brief history. *International Journal of Social Research Methodology*, 14(3), 179–189.
Fernandez, J. W. 1995. Egocentric particulars: Pronominal perspectives in ethnographic inquiry. *Beyond Textuality*, 303–326. https://doi.org/10.1515/9783110903010
Fleer, M. 2014a. A digital turn: Post-developmental methodologies for researching with young children. In: M. Fleer and A. Ridgway, eds. *Visual methodologies and digital tools for researching with young children: Transforming visuality*. New York; Dordrecht; London: Springer, pp. 3–4.
Fleer, M. 2014b. Beyond developmental geology: A cultural-historical theorisation of digital visual technologies for studying young children's development. In: M. Fleer and A. Ridgway, eds. *Visual methodologies and digital tools for researching with young children: Transforming visuality*. New York; Dordrecht; London: Springer, pp. 15–34.
Fleer, M. and Ridgway, A., eds, 2014. *Visual methodologies and digital tools for researching with young children: Transforming visuality*. New York, Dordrecht, London: Springer Link.
Fransberg, M., Myllylä, M. and Tolonen, J. 2021. Embodied graffiti and street art research. *Qualitative Research*. Available from: https://doi.org/10.1177/1468794 1211028795
Geertz, C. 1973. Thick description: Towards an interpretive theory of culture. In: C. Geertz, ed. *The interpretation of cultures*. New York: Basic Books.
Gold, S. J. 2007. Using photography in studies of immigrant communities. In: G. C. Stanczak, ed. *Visual research methods: Image, society and representation*. Thousand oaks, CA: SAGE.
Government of India, 2011. *Integrated Child Development Services (ICDS) scheme*. Ministry of Women & Child Development. New Delhi: Government of India.
Gragnolati. M., M. Shekar., D. Gupta., Bredenkam, C. and Lee, Y. 2005. *India's undernourished children: A call for reform and action*. (Health, Nutrition and Population, Discussion Paper). The World Bank: Washington DC.

Gu, L. 2017. Using school websites for home-school communication and parental involvement? *Nordic Journal of Studies in Educational Policy*, 3(2), 133–143. Available from: https://doi.org/10.1080/20020317.2017.1338498

Hammersley, M. 1999. Not bricolage but boat building: Exploring two metaphors for thinking about ethnography. *Journal of Contemporary Ethnography*, 28, 574–585.

Hammersley, M. 2006. Ethnography: Problems and prospects. *Ethnography and Education*, 1(1), 3–14.

Hammersley, M. and Atkinson, P. 2019. Ethnography in the digital world. *Ethnography: Principles in practice*. 4th ed. London; New York: Routledge, Taylor & Francis Group. Chapter 7: 139–151.

Haw, K. and Hadfield, M. 2011. *Video in social science research: Functions and forms*. London: Routledge.

Hedegaard, M. 2008. A cultural-historical theory of children's development. In: M. Hedegaard and M. Fleer, eds. *Studying children. A cultural-historical approach*. London: Open University Press, pp. 10–29.

Hedegaard, M. and Fleer, M. 2008. *Studying children. A cultural-historical approach*. London: Open University Press.

Hegel, G. W. F. 1969. *Science of logic*. London; New York: George Allen & Unwin Ltd.

Hegel, G. W. F. 1977. *Phenomenology of spirit*. Oxford: Oxford University Press. (First published 1807).

Henley, P. 2007. British ethnographic film: Recent developments. *Anthropology Today*, 19(1), 5–17.

Henley, P. 2010. Seeing, hearing, feeling: Sound and the despotism of the eye in 'visual' anthropology. In: I. Gunnar and J. K. Simonsen, eds. *Beyond the visual: Sound and image in ethnographic and documentary film*. Denmark: Intervention press.

Hine, C. 2000. *Virtual ethnography*. London: SAGE.

Hoadley, U. 2006. Analyzing pedagogy: The problem of framing. *Journal of Education*, 40, 15–34.

Hopwood, N. and Gottschalk, B. 2017. Double Stimulation 'in the wild': Services for families with children at-risk. *Learning, Culture and Social Interaction*, 13, 23–37.

Kearney, K. S. and Hyle, A. E. 2004. Drawing out emotions: The use of participant-produced drawings in qualitative inquiry. *Qualitative Research*, 4(3), 361–382.

Kemmis, S. and McTaggart, R. 2005. Participatory action research: Communicative action and the public sphere. In: N. K. Denzin and Y. S. Lincoln, eds. *The Sage handbook of qualitative research*. Thousand Oaks: SAGE Publications Ltd, pp. 559–603.

Knowles, C. and Sweetman, P. eds. 2004. *Picturing the social landscape: Visual methods and the sociological imagination*. London: Routledge.

Kress, G. 2003. *Literacy in the new media age*. London: Psychology Press.

Kress, G. 2010. *Multimodality: A social semiotic approach to contemporary communication*. Abingdon: Routledge.

Kress, G. 2012. Thinking about the notion of 'cross-cultural' from a social semiotic perspective. *Language and Intercultural Communication*, 12(4), 369–385.

Kress, G. and Burn, A. 2005. Pictures from a rocket: English and the semiotic take. *English Teaching: Practice and Critique*, 4(1), 95–106.

References

Lacey, C. 1970. *Hightown grammar*. Manchester: Manchester University Press.
Lambart, A. 1976. The sisterhood. In M. Hammersley and P. Woods eds., *The process of schooling*. London: Routledge and Kegan Paul.
Lambart, A. 1982. Expulsion in context: A school as a system in action. In R. Frankenberg ed., *Custom and conflict in british society*. Manchester: Manchester University Press.
Lambart, A. 1997. Mereside: A grammar school for girls in the 1960s. *Gender and Education*, 9, 441–456.
Langemeyer, I. and Roth, W.M. 2006. Is cultural-historical activity theory threatened to fall short of its own principles and possibilities as a dialectical social science?. *Outlines. Critical Practice Studies*, 8(2), 20–42.
Latour, B. and Woolgar, S. 1979. *Laboratory life: The Social construction of scientific facts*. Princeton, NJ: Princeton University Press.
Leont'ev, A. N. 1978. *Activity, consciousness, and personality*. (M. J. Hall, Trans). Englewood Cliffs, NJ: Prentice-Hall.
Leont'ev, A. N. 1932/1994. The development of voluntary attention in the child. In: R. Van der Veer and J. Valsiner, eds. *The Vygotsky reader*. Oxford: Blackwell, pp. 289–312.
Levinas, E. 1992. The face. *Ethics and infinity: Conversations with Phillippe Nemo* (trans. Richard A. Cohen). Pittsburgh: Duquesne University Press, pp. 83–92.
Levinas, E. 1999. *Alterity and transcendence* (trans Michael Smith). London: The Athlone Press.
Lincoln, Y. S. and Denzin, N. K. 2005. The eighth and ninth moments—Qualitative research in/and the fractured future. In: N. Denzin and Y. S. Lincoln, eds. *The Sage handbook of qualitative research*. 3rd ed. Thousand Oaks, CA: SAGE, 1115–1126.
Lipponen, L., Rajala, A., Hilppö, J. and Paananen. M. 2016. Exploring the foundations of visual methods used in research with children. *European Early Childhood Education Research Journal*, 24(6), 936–946.
Malinowski, B. 1922/2014. *Argonauts of the Western Pacific*. London: Routledge.
Marcus, G. E. and Fischer, M. M. J. 1986. *Anthropology as cultural critique: An experimental moment in the human sciences*. Chicago: University of Chicago Press.
Marx, K. 1973. *Grundrisse: Foundations of the critique of political economy* (Rough Draft). Harmondsworth: Penguin Books.
Mason, J. 2006. Mixing methods in a qualitatively driven way. *Qualitative Research*, 6(1), 9–25. Available from: https://doi.org/10.1177/1468794106058866
McNess, E., Arthur, L. and Crossley, M. 2015. 'Ethnographic dazzle' and the construction of the 'Other': Revisiting dimensions of insider and outsider research for international and comparative education. *Compare: A Journal of Comparative and International Education*, 45(2), 295–316.
McNiff, J. 2016. *You and your action research project*. London: Routledge.
Mead, M. 1975. Visual Anthropology in a discipline of words. In: P. Hockings, ed. *Principles of visual anthropology*. The Hague: Mouton Publishers, pp. 3–10.
Miller, R. 2011. *Vygotsky in perspective*. New York: Cambridge.
Milligan, L. 2014. Insider-outsider-inbetweener? Researcher positioning, participative methods and cross-cultural educational research. *Compare: A Journal of Comparative and International Education*. Available from: http://doi.org/10.1080/03057925.2014.928510
Mills, C. W. 1959. *The sociological imagination*. Oxford: Oxford University Press.

References

Moore, A., Wozniak, M., Yousef, A., Barnes, C. C., Cha, D., Courchesne, E. and Pierce, K. 2018. The geometric preference subtype in ASD: Identifying a consistent, early-emerging phenomenon through eye tracking. *Mol Autism*, 9(19), 1–13.

Moore, R. 2004. *Education and Society: Issues and explanations in the sociology of education.* Cambridge: Polity.

Moore, R. 2013. *Basil Bernstein: The thinker and the field.* London: Routledge.

Morais, A. and Neves, I. 2001. Pedagogic social contexts: Studies for a sociology of learning. In: A. Morais, I. Neves, B. Davies and H. Daniels, eds. *Towards a sociology of pedagogy: The contribution of Basil Bernstein to research.* New York: Peter Lang, pp. 185–221.

Morselli, D. and Sannino, A. 2021. Testing the model of double stimulation in a change laboratory. *Teaching and teacher education*, 97, 103224.

Moss, J. 2013. Visual research methods in education: In between difference and indifference. *International Journal on School Disaffection*, 10(2), 63–77.

Nyambe, J. and Wilmot, D. 2008. Bernstein's theory of pedagogic discourse: A framework for understanding how teacher educators in a Namibian college of education interpret and practice learner-centred pedagogy. Available from: http://www.caerdydd.ac.uk/socsi/newsandevents/events/Bernstein/papers/JohnNyambe.doc

Peters, R. S. 1966. *Ethics and education.* London: Allen and Unwin.

Pink, S. 2007. *Doing visual ethnography: Images, media and representation in research.* 2nd ed. London: SAGE.

Pink, S. 2013. *Doing visual ethnography.* 3rd ed. London: SAGE.

Pink, S. 2015. *Doing sensory ethnography.* 2nd ed. Los Angeles, CA; London: SAGE.

Pink, S. 2021. *Doing visual ethnography.* 4th ed. London: SAGE.

Pink, S., Ardèvol, E. and Lanzeni, D., eds. 2016. *Digital materialities: Design and anthropology.* 1st ed. London: Routledge.

Pink, S. and Hjorth, L. 2014. The digital wayfarer: Reconceptualising camera phone practices in an age of locomotive media. *Media International Australia*, 145(1): 145–155.

Pole, C., ed. 2004. *Seeing is believing? Approaches to visual research: Studies in qualitative methodology*, Volume 7. Oxford: Elsevier.

Pole, C. and Morrison, M. 2003. *Ethnography for education.* Maidenhead: McGraw-Hill Education.

Power, S. and G. Whitty. 2008. *A Bernsteinian analysis of compensatory education.* Working paper presented at the 5th Basil Bernstein Symposium, Cardiff University, July 9–12.

Prosser, J. 1998. *Image-based research. A sourcebook for qualitative researchers.* London: Falmer Press.

Prosser, J. and Loxley, A. 2008. *Introducing Visual Methods.* (ESRC National Centre for Research Methods Review Paper NCRM/010).

Qvortrup, J. 1994. Childhood matters: An introduction. In: J. Qvortrup, M. Bardy, G. Sgritta and H. Wintersberger, eds. *Childhood matters. Social theory, practice and politics.* Avebury: Aldershot, pp. 1–24.

Rainio, A. P. 2010. Lionhearts of the playworld. An ethnographic case study of the development of agency in play pedagogy. *Studies in Educational Sciences*, 233, Institute of Behavioural Sciences: University of Helsinki.

Rainio, A. P. and Hilppö, J. 2017. The dialectics of agency in educational ethnography. *Ethnography and Education*, 12(1), 78–94.

References

Rappoport, L. 1975. On praxis and quasi-rationality. *Human Development*, 18, 94–204.
Ridgway, A., Li, L. and Quiñones, G. 2016. Visual narrative methodology in educational research with babies: Triadic play in babies' room. *Video Journal of Education and Pedagogy*, 1(1), 1–18.
Riegel, K. F. 1973. Dialectic operations: The final period of cognitive development. *Human Development*, 16, 346–370.
Riegel. K. F. 1979. *Foundations of dialectical psychology*. New York: Academic Press.
Rose, G. 2013. On the relation between 'visual research methods' and 'contemporary visual culture'. *Sociological Review*. [Online]. Available from: http://onlinelibrary.wiley.com/doi/10.1111/1467-954X.12109/ abstract
Rose, G. 2016. *Visual methodologies: An introduction to researching with visual materials*. 4th ed. London: SAGE.
Rose, M. 2017. John Berger's ways of seeing & reading Magritte. Artblog. Available from: https://www.theartblog.org/2017/02/john-bergers-ways-of-seeing-reading-magritte/
Sadovnik, A. R. 2001. Basil Bernstein. *Prospects: The Quarterly Review of Comparative Education*, 31(4), 687–703.
Sannino, A. 2010. Teachers' talk of experiencing: Conflict, resistance and agency. *Teaching and Teacher Education*, 26(4), 838–844.
Sannino, A. 2011. Activity theory as an activist and interventionist theory. *Theory & Psychology*, 21(5), 571–597.
Sannino, A. 2015a. The principle of double stimulation: A path to volitional action. *Learning Culture and Social Interaction*, 6, 1–15.
Sannino, A. 2015b. The emergence of transformative agency and double stimulation: Activity-based studies in the Vygotskian tradition. *Learning, Culture and Social Interaction*, 4, 1–3.
Sannino, A., Engeström, Y. and Lemos, M. 2016. Formative interventions for expansive learning and transformative agency. *Journal of the Learning Sciences*, 25(4), 599–633.
Sannino, A. and Laitinen, A. 2015. Double stimulation in the waiting experiment: Testing a Vygotskian model of the emergence of volitional action. *Learning, Culture, and Social Interaction*, 4, 4–18.
Spante, M., Varga, A. and Carlsson, L. 2022. Triggering sustainable professional agency: Using change laboratory to tackle unequal access to educational success collectively. *Journal of Workplace Learning*, 34(2), 162–175.
Spinuzzi, C. 2020. Trying to predict the future: Third-generation activity theory's codesign orientation. *Mind, Culture, and Activity*, 27(1), 4–18.
Teräs, M. and Lasonen, J. 2013. The development of teachers' intercultural competence using a change laboratory method. *Vocations and Learning*, 6(1), 107–134.
Thomson, P., ed. 2008. *Doing visual research with children and young people*. New York and London: Routledge.
Thorne, S. L. 2015. Mediated life activity, double stimulation, and the question of agency. *Learning, Culture and Social Interaction*, 4, 62–66.
Tobin, J., Hsueh, Y. and Karasawa, M. 2009. *Preschool in three cultures revisited: China, Japan, and the United States*. Chicago: The University of Chicago Press.
Tolman. 2001. The origins of activity as a category in the philosophies of Kant, Fichte, Hegel and Marx. In S. Chaiklin, ed. *The theory and practice of cultural historical psychology*. Denmark: Aarhus University Press, pp. 84–92.

Toohey, K. and Smythe, S. 2022. A different difference in teacher education: Posthuman and decolonizing perspectives, *Language and Education*, 36(2), 122–136.

Tversky, B. 2019. *Mind in motion: How action shapes thought*. USA: Hachette.

Van der Veer, R. and Valsiner, J. 1991. *Understanding Vygotsky: A quest for synthesis*. Oxford: Blackwell.

Veresov, N. 2014. Method, methodology and methodological thinking. In: M. Fleer and A. Ridgway, eds. *Visual methodologies and digital tools for researching with young children: Transforming visuality*. New York; Dordrecht; London: Springer, pp. 215–288.

Virkkunen, J. and Newnham, D. S. 2013. Preparing and carrying out change laboratory sessions. *The change laboratory: A tool for collaborative development of work and education*. Springer science and business media. Rotterdam: Sense Publishers, pp. 79–116.

Vygotsky, L. S. 1929/1979. The development of higher forms of attention in childhood. *Journal of Russian and East European Psychology*, 18(1), 67–115.

Vygotsky, L. S. 1987. Thinking and speech. *The collected works of Vygotsky vol.1: Problems of general psychology*. Edited by R. W. Rieber and A. S. Carton, trans by N. Minick. New York: Plenum. (First published 1934)

Vygotsky, L. S. 1998a. Part 2: Problems of child (developmental) psychology. In: R. W. Rieber, ed. *The collected works, volume 5, child psychology*. New York: Plenum, pp. 187–296.

Vygotsky, L. S. 1998b. Early childhood. In: R. W. Rieber, ed. *The collected works, volume 5, child psychology*. New York: Plenum, pp. 319–333.

Vygotsky, L. S. and Cole, M. 1978. *Mind in society: Development of higher psychological processes*. Cambridge, MA; London: Harvard University Press.

Waermö, M. 2016. Broadening rules and aligning actions: Children's negotiation while playing hide-and-seek during break time. *Learning, Culture and Social Interaction*, 11, 9–28.

Wagner, J. 2001. Does image-based field work have more to gain from extending or from rejecting scientific realism? An essay in review. *Visual Sociology*, 16(2), 7–21.

Wagner, J. 2006. Visible materials, visualised theory and images of social research. *Visual Studies*, 21(1), 55–69.

Wang, C. and Burris, M. A. 1994. Empowerment through Photo Novella portraits of participation. *Heaflth Education and Behaviour* 21, 171–186.

Watson, J. D. 1968. *The double helix: A personal account of the discovery of the structure of DNA*. New York: Atheneum.

Wax, R. H. 1971. *Doing fieldwork: Warnings and advice*. Chicago: The University of Chicago Press.

Webb, E. J., Campbell, D. T., Schwartz, R. D. and Sechrest, L. 1966. *Unobtrusive measures: Nonreactive research in the social sciences*. Chicago: Rand McNally.

Wertsch, J., Tulviste, P. and Hagstrom. F. 1996. A sociocultural approach to agency. In: E. Forman, N. Minick and C. Stone, eds. *Contexts for learning - Sociocultural dynamics in children's development*. New York: Oxford University Press, pp. 336–356.

Willis, P. 1977. *Learning to labour: How working class kids get working class jobs*. Farnborough: Saxon House. Reprint by Columbia University Press (1 Dec. 1981).

Index

Note: Pages in *italics* refer to figures, pages in **bold** refer to tables, and pages followed by n refer to notes.

action research 90; as an intervention approach 90; Change Laboratory *vs.* 91–92
activity system: analysis of 95–96; Change Laboratory and 91–92, *92*; contradictions of *92*, 92–93; Leont'ev's 115; practitioners 100–101
adult–child interactions 6, 69
age 13
Alexander, R. 67
Anganwadi Centers (AWCs), Mumbai 47, 121; *see also* Integrated Child Development Services; background settings of 57–58; case studies 58–66, *59–66*
anganwadi worker (AWW) 58
apprenticeship approach 67
AT diagram 124–125; Engeström's 102–104, 124; ideas screen and 104–105; mirror and ideas screens 107; mirror data as 105–106; mirror screen as 105–106; social context and knowledge construction 102–104; visual representation of 104, 115
AT framework 99
AT theory 101

Balinese society 1
Banks, M. 124–125
Bateson, G. 1
Becker, H. S. 1, 17
Berger, J. 4–5
Bernstein, B. 8, 46–48; 'language of description' in anganwadi and 66–67; basis of pedagogic practice 51–52; classification and framing 49–51; combining theory and method 56–66; and pedagogic discourse 49; theory of invisible/visible pedagogy 48
Blunden, A. 92, 118n2
body gestures 56
body positioning 56
Bruner's theory of imitative learning 67
Burgess, R. G. 5–6

Cartesian model 44
Change Laboratory (CL): action research *vs.* 91–92; activity system and 91–92, *92*; as a collaborative visual language of description 115–118; intervention methodology 6, 90–96; methodology 115–118; object-oriented activity of

92–94; transformation in work 89; visual representations in 89–118
child as learner 49–51
child-centred education, notion of 67
child-centred pedagogy 47, 67–68
child–child relations 63, 67
childhood ethnography 22, *22–31*
childhood researchers, video modalities of 71–72
China, pre-school pedagogy in 71–72
claim 22
class 13
collaborative representation 125
collective object 94
Collier, J. 1, 18–20, 34
Collier, J. C., Jr. 17
Collier, M. 18–20, 34
common object 98–99
communication: cultural technologies of 121; facial expressions to, power of 123; modes of 120; non-verbal 56; pedagogic 55–67; practitioner–child 57; social theory of 120; verbal 55
conflicts 96
context 13, 39
COVID-19, impact of 16
crisis of representation 21–22
cultural historical activity theory tradition (CHAT) 89–91, 94, 96–101; *see also* Change Laboratory
cultural product, social functions of 2–3
cultural technologies of communication 121
cultural-historical psychology of education 44
culture 10–11; dynamic view of 11; informal and formal interview 11; participant and non-participant 11
curriculum language 39
cycle of expansive learning 94, 98

'decoding of reality' 5
data collection: and analysis 98–101; in fieldwork 11; process 20; in video modalities *37–38*, 38–40, 57, 73; visual methods of 6, 34
Denzin, N. K. 21, 127
development work research (DWR) methodology 90, 99–101, **100**, 124–125; AT diagram 102–104; researcher as interventionist in 104–105
dialectical concept of agency, notion of 86–87
dialectical epistemological position 41
dialectics: application in visual technology 42; conditions through father–child interactions 72–75; contradictions 41; and development as change 43–44; in ethnographic knowledge 40–45; ethnography and **43**; framework 75, 86; human development and 41–44; logic in Hegelian/Marxian sense 40; ontology 92–93, 124; person-social/ societal 70; relational 40; Riegel's framework of 41–42; roots of 40; in social world 41; theory, applications of 40–45; in visual contexts 40–45; in visual technology 42, 44
digital cameras 2
'digital materiality' 126–127
digital photographs of blackboards 47
'digital wayfarer' 126
discursive rules 49, 56, 59, 62, 66
DNA structure 6
documentary photography 22
double stimulation 90; theory of 83–84; value of 84–85
dualism 44

Early Childhood Education 52
educational practice, change in 89

empirical analysis 96
Engeström, Y. 91, 94–97; AT triangle diagram 91, 102
England 90, 97–98; video modalities in 72, 82–85
epistemological theory 49
ethnicity 13
ethnographers: role as photographers 34; subjectivity 15
ethnographic dimensions 12
ethnographic knowledge 12–13, 15, 18; dialectics in 40–45; new routes to 32–43
'ethnographic' orientated phase 99
ethnographic research 1; being reflexive in 32–43
ethnographic truth 19–20; see also truth
ethnographic-oriented research 128
ethnographicness 14–15
ethnography: approach 11–12; characterising 14; childhood 22; conceptualisation of 12; context and holism in 13; defining the term 11–12; development of 'experience-rich' 57; of educational settings 11; longitudinal information in 11; as methodological approach 13–14; as a reflexive 33; similarities between dialectics and **43**; virtual 16
expansive developmental research methodology 95–96; empirical analysis 96; historical analysis 95–96; object historical analysis 95
expansive learning 90; theory of 95
extraction video modalities 71, 73–75; case study 75–87, *76–77*

facial expressions 122
family activity settings 72–73
father–child interactions 69, 72–75
Father Groups 90, 97–98
Fischer, M. 21

Fleer, M. 72–74
fluid visual modality 120
'futures-oriented' approach 126

gender 13
GoPro cameras 35–40
Govandi project 58; *see also* Anganwadi Centers (AWCs), Mumbai; case studies 58–66, *59–66*

Hadfield, M. 70–71
Hargreaves, D. 10
Haw, K. 70–71
Hedegaard, M. 72
Hegel, G. W. F. 40, 74
Henley, P. 39, 57
Hilppö, J. 40–41, 74
Hinduism 67
historical analysis 95–96
historico-genetic method 96
holism 13
Hong Kong, video modalities in 72, 78–81, *79–81*
human activity 91
human development 69; dialectics and 41–44

image analysis, internal narrative of 56–57
India: Anganwadi Centers, Mumbai 58–66, *59–66*; research-related activities in 54; video modalities in 72
informed consent 122
institutional culture 94–95
instructional context 56
Integrated Child Development Services (ICDS) 46–47; *see also* Anganwadi Centers (AWCs), Mumbai; combining visual data with other data collection methods and 54–55; documentation 67; logging, editing and sampling visual material 55; methodological issues in 47–48; modalities of pedagogic practice and 51–52;

as non-functional and uneven 53; pedagogic discourse, classification and framing of 49–51; pre-school component of 48; Pre-School Education and 52; settings 53; structural issues in 54; in urban areas 53
intervention approach: action research as an 90; Change Laboratory as an 90–96
invisible pedagogy: description of 46–47; visual technology and 46–68

Japan, pre-school pedagogy in 71

Kress, G. 120–121, 124–125, 127

Lacey, C. 10
Lambart, A. 10
language 55, 120; curriculum 39; development 61
learner agency 84–87
learner-centred pedagogy 48
learning: in formal schooling 22; at work 89
'language of description' 66, 68
'Learning to Labour' 10
Leont'ev, A. N. 91, 118n6
Levinas, E. 122
Lincoln, Y. S. 21, 127
Lipponen, L. 72
lived experiences of people 22, *22–31*
longitudinal information in ethnography 11

Magritte, R. 4–5
Malinowski, B. 11
Marcus, G. 21
Marx, K. 40
Mead, M. 1, 17–18
mental rotation 117
mirror data 101; as AT diagram 105–106
mirror screen 101; as AT diagram 105–106
modalities of pedagogic practice 51–52

modes of communication 120
Moss, J. 125–126
MS Teams 16

Newnham, D. S. 111, 116
non-verbal communication 56
Norway, video modalities in 72, 76–78, *77*

object historical analysis 95
object-oriented activity 92–94; sampling strategy of 98
objective reality 4
objectivity, classic norms of 22
ontological positions 21
ontological theory 49
open-ended research 11
Otavalo Indians 19

pedagogic communication: structures of 56–57; theoretical analysis of 67; visual analysis and 57–66
pedagogic discourse: classification and framing of 49–51; through visual research method 49–55
pedagogic practice, basis of 51–52
pedagogic relationship, questions and context related to 39
person-social/ societal dialectic 70
personal relationships 41
Peters, R.S. 42
photo elicitation *22–31*; interviews 54
photo voice 71–72
photographing technology 19; politics and power relations in 34; weaving culture of Otavalo Indians and 19–21
Pink, S. 14, 18–20, 34, 126–128
'Point of view' (PoV) 45n1
Pole, C. 14
policy documentation 97
post-human new materialism 127
'post-modern like' deconstruction 33
practitioner–child communication 57
practitioner–child relations 67

practitioners, as transmitters 59
praxis 45n2
pre-school culture 46
Pre-School Education (PSE) 52; component 52–53
pre-school pedagogy 71
'Pre-School in Three Cultures Study' 71
principle of volition 84
problem solving 94
process *vs.* product 14–15
professional collaborative learning 89
Prosser, J. 34

qualitative research, in USA 21
qualitative researchers 21
qualitative transformation 85

The Race for the Double Helix (1987) 5–6
Rainio, A. P. 40–41, 74
receivers 54
reflection video modalities 71, 73–75, 85; case study 75–87, *76–77*
reflexive: questions 33; in visual research 32–44
reflexivity 33; concept of 15; problem of 15; from Woodland Walk scene 35–40, *37–38*
regulative rules 49
relational dialectics 40
religion 13
re-mediation, principles of 90
replicability 18
representations 71
're-presentations' of reality 33, 45
researcher positionality 54–55
researcher-interventionist, role of: facilitating a 'transformation of the activity' as 111–115, *114*; facilitating expansive learning actions as 108–111, *110*; facilitating knowledge construction as 107–108
researcher, as interventionist 104–105

Ridgway, A. 72
Riegel, K. F. 41–42
'The role of theory in field research' 5
rules of criteria (evaluation) 49

Sannino, A. 84
scientific realism: approaches to documentary photography 22; content of images and 18; context and its narration of events 18–32; visual representation and 18–32
second generation CHAT (2 GAT) 92
self-discipline 67
self-regulation 67
semi-structured interviews 57
Smythe, S. 127–128
social anthropology 10
social reality 10, 16; notions of truth about 17; visual representation and 17–40
social science research, video modalities in 4, 70–72
social semiotic theory 120
social theory of communication 120
social/educational research 21
socio-cultural anthropology 10
socio-economic status 98
Spinuzzi, C. 115
student-student relations 56
subject–object interdependence 12–13
subjective reality of human beings 10
Sure Start 90, 97, 118n1

teacher-student relations 56
technology and knowledge 39
theory of double stimulation 83–84
Tobin, J. 71
Toohey, K. 127–128
transformative visual representation 125
transmitters 54

truth 4–5, 19; about social reality 44–45; dialectic 40; ethnographic 20
Tversky, B. 117

unit of analysis 91–92
USA, pre-school pedagogy in 71

value, of double stimulation 84–85
video analysis, experiential characteristic of 56–57
video extracts, commenting on 70
video methodology, international research team and 122–123, *123*
video modalities: case studies of 75–87, *76–77*, *79–81*; for childhood researchers 71–72; data collection in 73; in England 72, 82–85; ethics 75; extractive 71, 75–87, *76–77*, *79–81*; in Hong Kong 72, 78–81, *79–81*; implications for 85–87; in India 72; in Norway 72, 76–78, *77*; as a psychological technique 69–88; reflective 71, 75–87, *76–77*, *79–81*; role of theory in 73–75; in social science research 70–72
videotaping 101
Virkkunen, J. 111, 116
virtual ethnography 16
visual ambiguity 32–43; problem of 34–35
Visual Anthropology: Photography as a Research Method (1967) 1
'visible' behaviours 71
visual contexts, dialectics in 40–45
visual cultures, in photographic documentation 35

visual data 46; combining with other data collection 54–55; researcher-generated 51, 68; as a way of gaining orientation 68
visual footage, teachers' reflections on 38
visual material, logging, editing and sampling 55
visual modes and modalities 2–3, **3**
visual representation 33; scientific realism and 18–32; social reality and 17–40; visual cultures and 35
visual representations: in Change Laboratory 89–118; and screens 101–107
visual research method: being reflexive in 32–43; pedagogic cultures through 49–55
visual technologies 1–2, 121–122; for educational ethnography 6, 17–45; and forms of potential visual data 6
Visual technology, dialectics in 42, 44
Vygotsky, L. S. 91; zone of proximal development 91, 94–95

Wagner, J. 34
'Ways of Seeing' 4
weaving: culture of Otavalo Indians, photographing technology and 19–21; elements of 21
web-based sources 2
Willis, P. 10
Woodland Walk *37–38*
work-based learning 89

zone of proximal development (ZPD) 91, 94–95
Zoom 16

For Product Safety Concerns and Information please contact our EU representative GPSR@taylorandfrancis.com
Taylor & Francis Verlag GmbH, Kaufingerstraße 24, 80331 München, Germany

www.ingramcontent.com/pod-product-compliance
Lightning Source LLC
Chambersburg PA
CBHW071507150426
43191CB00009B/1439